LOVE & JUSTICE
A Compelling True Story Of Triumph Over Tragedy

Diana Morgan-Hill

blackbird

Published by Blackbird Digital Books, London
ISBN-13: 978993092237
Copyright: Diana Morgan-Hill 2015
Cover Design by Fena Lee www.pheeena.carbonmade.com

MOR

This book is dedicated to:

Agnes Veen Hill – my wonderful Mama, and best friend
and
Lara Morgan-Hill – my beloved daughter, you are my life's most
precious gift

INTRODUCTION

Fragile

The last time I ran was for a train.

It was a warm August evening and a slight breeze fanned my face as I strolled into the safe, suburban railway station just outside London. A few straggling commuters huddled at the ticket kiosk. Realising the train was pulling in, I hurried across the bridge, scurried down the stairs, quickly and evenly, dashed across the platform and raised my leg to get on the train.

The door was open, I was on the running board and aware of people inside the carriage. Suddenly the train jerked and I lost my grip on the inside of the door. The train jolted again and I lost my balance. The weight of the heavy bag on my shoulder tipped me backwards and I dropped.

With a wrench, the sudden movement twisted me round and crushed me down. As I became wedged at chest-height between the train and the platform, the train picked up speed. I screamed and screamed and grasped desperately at the concrete. But the train dragged me along, gaining momentum, crushing my ribs against the platform, until I fell into the darkness and the wheels below.

One of my legs was ripped off, just below the knee. Beyond saving, my other leg was amputated above the knee later that night.

In 7 seconds I went from busy girl about international town businesswoman with everything to live for to a double-amputee, my life in ruins.

What could be worse? Could there be anything worse?

Well, yes.

Seven days after my accident as I lay in a hospital bed traumatised and heavily sedated with painkillers, I learnt in the most underhand way imaginable that British Rail were going to interview me with a view to prosecution for trespassing onto their railway line.

It was unfathomable. I couldn't yet believe what had happened.

That a train would move off as passengers were still getting onto it?

That the train would then not be stopped immediately by the Guard?

That I had just lost both of my legs for crying out loud. It simply couldn't be true. But it was, and so the parallel nightmare began.

An indicator as to how British Rail would be behaving came just days after the accident. Their chosen method of communication was not by any letter or phone call to myself or to my dear, traumatised relatives, but, whilst we were all still in deepest shock, via the newspapers. There it was in black and white for all of London, and then as the news spread, the nation, to see: British Rail were going to employ a 100 year old bye-law and prosecute me for trespassing onto their railway line.

This was the first aggressive tactic by British Rail to throw the authorities off the real scent. They then chose to fight me. In every undermining way their highly-paid team of lawyers could possibly conjure up. There followed an exhaustive mission by myself, my family, friends and lawyers to follow this repugnant trail and clear my name. The legal battle that ensued took away five years of my life at a time when I was trying to learn to live again in the most painful ways imaginable.

When I look back on those years I can say with all honesty that my fight with British Rail is the worst thing that has ever happened to me. Yes, even worse than having both my legs stolen from me. This attitude, of a public corporation towards its passengers was, at first, hard to fathom. But as, along with learning to live without legs, I embarked on my legal battle, the reasoning behind their inhumane methodology soon clarified.

CHAPTER ONE

7 Seconds

After a busy morning, I'd left my business partner, Sarah, in the West End to tie up the details on another Primetime meeting, and had raced back to our office to prepare the paperwork needed by a new client that afternoon.

MediaVision was based in an attic bedroom in Sarah and Justin's Wandsworth semi in a safely suburban street 4 miles or so from central London. An arrangement we kept carefully hidden from the majority of our clients with their palatial, glassy offices in downtown New York, LA and Paris.

I was due to meet fellow PR Barbie back in town for pre-dinner drinks and moved speedily around the office, darting backwards and forwards between the filing cabinets and my computer. Yellow Post-it stickers littered the circumference of the screen – messages from Max, a tall, blue-eyed blonde American I'd met at the annual MIP Media Conference in Cannes and fallen for in a big way. When I discovered he was taken I'd finished it but he was still in hot pursuit. So far I'd been fortunate in that Sarah had been there to pick up the phone when he'd called. Though I'd finally moved on I didn't want the temptation. Even his voice was dangerous – heavy in maturity and sexuality.

Typing furiously, my eyes drifted out of the window to the sunny day. I thought about ice-cream, wondering if I'd have time to grab a cooling cone to eat on the train. I bounced my way down the narrow flights of stairs, stopping off at the hall mirror to reapply my eye-liner and lipstick. I was looking good, lean and healthy with a sexy real-tan glow, attained from a quick week away to Greece with best friend Dinah and her family at the end of July. I gave myself a little smile before slamming the heavy door behind me and setting off for the station.

Heat warped the afternoon air and I could hear a distant cooing from a summer dove. An endless chorus from twittering birds added further song to the radiated atmosphere of that hot, sunny afternoon. Dawdling by the post-box, I rummaged in the over-sized bag slung over my shoulder, ferreting for my rail-pass and letters to shove in the slot.

I walked quickly. My Walkman, attached to my trouser waistline, bumped slightly with each step. The headphones were around my neck. I preferred birdsong whilst I was out and about and didn't usually wear it until I was travelling to relieve the boredom of the long train commutes. I produced home-made tapes in my flat. The best songs from favourite albums got me frequently dancing around my home, the volume on the stereo turned up high.

All around were sights and sounds of an overcooked summer. Trees wilted with heat, leaves drooped with dust. An ice-cream van tinkled gently in the distance. I turned quickly into the station entrance, a blast of hotter diesel air greeting me from the hissing, squeaking train standing at platform one. When I got to the top of the stairs I saw through the bridge railings that my own train was trundling its 400 ton weight into the station. My cream, cropped top stuck slightly to my back as I readjusted the heavy bag on my shoulder and began trotting over the bridge.

A crowd of passengers hung around the glass box that caged the ticket collector. This was the fourth time I'd passed him that day. He filled the cubby hole, a black mass of shiny face and uniform. He seemed both distracted and sleepy. I didn't bother to flash the pass that was in my hand. I had to struggle through a crowd of dawdling, chattering passengers who appeared to have all the time in the world.

I knocked one of them with my bag. Sensing she was cross, I muttered a hurried apology, intent on catching my train. I quick-stepped down the stairs and across the platform. The door of the train wasn't fully closed and opened easily. I had my right foot on the running board and was raising the other when the train jerked ferociously. I made eye contact with some of the other passengers sitting inside the train. The train pulled away from me violently. I mouthed OH!

Then my right foot slipped, my hands scrabbled. As I clung to the wooden sides of the doorframe, the train jolted again. My left leg dropped below the running board. I struggled and was twisted down, down until I was wedged, crushed, between the train and the platform wall. Four hundred tons of metal began to roll against my back. The force rolled on, my feet were in the platform well, my stomach and chest pressed hard-up against the platform. I raised my hands, waiting for it to slow down and stop.

But the train didn't stop.

Instead, it speeded up.

Through fear rather than pain I screamed, 'Stop, stop the train!'

In a typically English way, I felt embarrassment. WHY didn't they see me?

A red terror gripped as I realised how much worse my predicament was becoming. I was pinned, a butterfly with all limbs mentally flailing, my feet were with the wheels, massive, heavy crushing wheels and the train was moving faster, faster. I was still relatively safe with the wall and, although flattened, I hugged it still closer to me. I thought very clearly, "Keep your head away from the train".

A metallic fear hit my nostrils and flooded my brain.

I felt a tugging and then – nothing.

My memory of the moment I fell beneath the wheels, thank God, does not exist.

I came out from the black pit of nothingness.

The train had stopped and I was trapped beneath it.

The smell of evil permeated the air, fumes of dust and black grimy coal. I breathed the gagging fumes of diesel and electricity.

A dull thud, atrocious in pain level, reached up from the track and held my body deadly still. I did not breathe, I did not move as the thud hit me again. Electricity was holding me down, claiming its route through my body, the fragile vessel. It made a sound, the deepest lowest buzzzz.

I raised my head from the ground, thinking, 'I've got to get up, I've got to get out of this.' A strange object came into focus, it lay away from my body at a distorted angle. A sliver of something attached it to me. What was it? It didn't look human. But I recognised the shoe. It was mine.

No. It couldn't be.

No.

This is not me.

A wretched agonising pain filled all of me instantly. If there was a Richter scale for pain, this would be a tornado, a major earthquake, shuddering through my body. A sickening weight was crushing my left leg. I couldn't see what caused it. My hands raked at the wall, my nails clawed the brick, I HAD to get up.

'Help me,' I mewed. 'Help me. This is not me,' I called from some primitive survival base in the back of my throat. I didn't recognise the voice. 'This is not happening to me. 'Help.' It was depleting my energy. I fell quiet. Too frightened to speak. But then came the surge of adrenalin, the adrenalin of fear and flight, my energy hopelessly boosted.

But there could be no flight. The fear accelerated.

A kind face appeared, warm black in colour. Soft eyes, sad eyes. He bent down. 'I'm so sorry, someone will help you. I am so sorry.' He straightened himself and left, walking backwards, his eyes registering horror.

Train doors slammed and banged. Panic rose. I sensed no one until Maggie appeared. I knew that was her name because I asked her and, even in fear and panic, one is polite.

'Diana, hold on. Don't worry.' She was desperately trying to give me some security. Some semblance of hope. But I didn't care. It wasn't me she was speaking to anyway. I didn't know where I'd gone. She held my hand. I gripped her life-force, unsure of where mine was.

Minutes ticked away, every second a tortuous hour of horror. A female policewoman type was there, on the edge of the platform. Her voice annoyed and distressed me. Two ambulance men arrived. They had difficulty getting to me. The train had to be moved. I could hear them talking. They'd have to switch the electricity on again to do that. It could give me an electric shock. The driver, sweating, heaving, tried to squeeze his way to me. He couldn't. I let go of Maggie's hand. I didn't want her to be there when they moved the train off me if that electricity hit again. I knew I wouldn't survive a third jolt of 650 volts. I put my head down on the track and scratched my nails deep into the black coal, perfect shiny pink against black. I remembered painting them that morning so they'd look beautiful.

That was a time long distant. Another, parallel, universe had taken me over.

Oblivion, that's what I craved and that was the vision before me. If I turned my head away from the platform, to the left and to the tracks, that was all I could see – oblivion, an all-enveloping sense of being nothing. Not existing in any form. If I turned my head to the right, and raised it slightly I could see Maggie. I could reach my hand up to her. I chose to take her hand as they rolled the train off me.

I heard the engine of the train and buried my face into the stones of the track. Give me that oblivion. I was groaning and the sounds I made frightened me.

'Don't do this. Don't do this to me.'

'Diana give me your hand. Please Diana, give me your hand.' Maggie ignored the wishes of the forces around her. They were concerned about the amount of electricity required to move the train. I couldn't bear it. I turned my head to the left, away from the platform, away from Maggie. But the oblivion I faced seemed too deep. Too uncomprehending. Was this death?

I heard Maggie's soft voice again, pleading with me to turn to her. I obeyed and took her hand as they rolled the train off my left leg.

With trembling voices and gentle hands they put, what seemed to be, plastic bags on my legs.

'I'm sorry love, we need a doctor for painkillers,' said one, his voice so low, so timorous, I could barely hear it. But I hadn't asked for painkillers. I pleaded for a direct blow to the head from a sledgehammer. I whimpered the request, like a puppy in severe pain.

When you are in pain, a pain that obliterates everything else, you don't scream, you squeal quietly, conserving energy.

A policewoman stood over me, looking in my bag. Her voice, strangely, got on my nerves. 'Who should we contact?' she asked. My first thoughts were my mum and dad. I couldn't do this to them, not after Dad's accident.

'Sister. Helen. Drew. Drew,' I whimpered half of Andrew's name twice.

'An... Drew. I need him. Please. Sur Name Palmer.'

I couldn't breathe. My parents, oh sweet Jesus, Mum and Dad. I couldn't think of anything. Such pain obliterates most thoughts, my brain didn't work. My eyes couldn't see anything.

'Contact lenses. I wear contact lenses. Tell the surgeons I wear contact lenses.'

The ambulance men moved fast, attaching drips, which I could see, and doing something with my legs, which I couldn't. Their breathing was heavy, I pleaded again to be knocked out. 'Sledgehammer' I muttered, over and over.

I could smell the sweat on them, it reeked of distress.

Somehow they got me onto a portable stretcher. Somehow they got me across four tracks and into the ambulance. I was shivering with shock, my teeth chattering and clacking with a fearful shuddering.

'They will sew it back on again, won't they?' I asked the poor sod who had to travel with me in the back of the vehicle.

'Don't worry about it love. Not now,' said the ambulance man, his words shaking away the enormity of the truth. I remembered the same cadence of voice from inside the ambulance that had taken Dad to hospital, a few weeks previously.

The kindly lie. A lie is kinder than the truth. For everyone.

I lay face down and remained face down when they took me out of the ambulance and through the swing doors to Accident and Emergency. I'd seen this on television. I was in an episode of ER.

White coats flapped. There seemed to be a room full of them.

Voices asked about my back. Scissors sheared material off my back. A slight piercing of indignation hit my senses. I like that shirt! What are you doing? I called again for a sledgehammer. I pleaded for the big hit over the head that would overrule all pain which had moved me from the real world into who knows what this was.

'Your back, Diana, does your back hurt?'

'No. Please knock me out, Doctor. Please.'

Still face down, I lifted my head slightly and looked straight ahead. There was one of the sweetest faces I'd ever seen. Another angel, looking distressed. A nurse with soft eyes. Deepest compassion.

'Breathe into this Diana.'

'Am I going to have a baby?' I muttered, ironic to the end. I gulped at the mask and I was gone.

I came to and Andrew stood at the end of the bed, looking at me, his pale face shadowed in gloom. I felt I must say something, sensing my last words had to be said now. It was not just him I delivered those three words to, they were for everyone close to me.

'I love you.'

'I love you too.' His words, reluctant, hoarse with fear.

I felt I could go, aware of my last exhalation as I fell away to the darkness.

CHAPTER TWO

Everybody Wants to Rule the World

I was becoming an addict. Not to the soothing opiates that my severely damaged body required, but to the past. The Diamorphine, providing a soothing path through the arterial highways and nestling in my brain, released visual other-worldly clips of me. What I had been and what I had done. Self-induced hallucination: I escaped whenever I could to my previous life, to the land of the now dead Diana. The memories were colourfully vivid, with a clarity only dreams can generate. Jasmine on a warming breeze. Sunlit sand kissed my feet. I walked to the water's edge.

Cannes
'Imagine the view from up there,' I murmured to the group of girlfriends scattered around me on the long stretch of manicured beach. We were looking at a mountain range to our right. Five peaks haloed by a haze of pink light unique to the South of France. I smiled at the beauty of the sun waltzing on the gentle azure of the sea.

A sound system lay beside us, peppered with grains of sand from our rigorous aerobic activity. I had chivvied the others through a half-hour routine, calling on them to pull up their knees, perform star jumps into the air and run on the spot, all in time to carefully selected non-stop rhythms.

I had devised the "keep-fit in Cannes" plan on the spur of the moment, the night before. The idea had not seemed too crazy then, pricking my brain with a rush of energy at 2.30 in the morning. I had been buoyed up with champagne cocktails and a television programme launch that had gone well. It had seemed the natural thing to do. By 7.30am, my head pulsing with a slight hangover, I regretted the scheme, but still I phoned the girls to remind them. At 8am I handed out extra large white T-shirts, splashed across the front with a bright green logo of my company,

MediaVision. By 8.15am Black Box's *Ride On Time* was blaring out of the speakers and we were well into the routine, producing endorphins for our bodies and publicity for my new company, a press and publicity service for the television industry. Our audience included four beach sweepers, a couple of miserable waiters who were putting out tables and chairs for the lunchtime sessions, and a number of key industry figures quick-stepping their way into the Palais for breakfast meetings. An ambitious start to another day in television hell!

The Palais du Festival, or the "bunker" as it's called by regulars, is the commercial castle of modern Cannes. It dominates the harbour, welcoming the famous, the rich, and the media peons. The gates to the Palais will be forever open to those who hold passes, costing upwards of £100 (around $148) per day. Cannes thrives as a media hot-spot, location for the most famous film festival in the world and is home twice a year to television and publishing executives attending events like MIP, the biggest international market for the sale of television and multimedia programmes.

For the previous three years I had attended trade exhibitions as a journalist, interviewing luminaries like David Puttnam, Silvio Berlusconi, Ted Turner, Robert Maxwell; Peter Gabriel and Bob Geldof. I had been working for different magazines, all exciting, tiring and addictive, but this was my first year at Cannes as MD of my own company. My ambition turbo-charged by 100% pure adrenalin.

As we danced and leapt about on the beach, above and behind us the famous Croisette pavements began to teem with life. Amongst the locals an invading army had begun to march. They appeared as if from nowhere. Tight suited women, their hair and make-up immaculate, high heeled and shoulder-padded their way into the Palais; men in sombre ties and plain coloured ensembles carried briefcases or bags displaying television logos. These were people dressed with a purpose and a mission – to buy or sell.

'Barbieeeeeee!' The screech pierced our blissful haven on the beach and all of us stopped dancing at the same time. Barbie clawed for her sweatshirt top and sunglasses, buried in the sand, and rushed off towards the woman yelling from the Croisette.

'She's late,' grinned Christine.

'And so are we,' announced Jane, looking at her watch.

We jogged back to our hotel, nodding to other "members" of the industry who looked surprised at our red, sweating faces.

'Are you still seeing Max?' asked Christine as we approached our small, basic hotel tucked away up a tiny back street.

'Dunno,' I answered quietly, feeling my stomach twitch at the sound of his name. He was perfect for me in all but one way. He was married.

I had met Max at my first market in Cannes three years previously. I'd fallen for the charms of Cannes on my first night and for Max on the second. My business partner Sarah had introduced us and then backed away as Max and I stood, smiling at each other. I had cheekily leaned over to him and commented on his dreadful tie (blue, yellow and purple swirls). His soft, sexy drawl had captured my interest and immediately planted the seeds of desire in my mind.

We saw each other perhaps five times a year – he lived in New York, I in London. I was madly in love with him. He was handsome, blonde, blue-eyed. He had a kind face, was tall and always dressed in beautiful well-cut suits ordered from a London tailor. Originally from Indiana, he was now a sophisticated and cultured New Yorker. He was the consummate gentleman and I smiled to myself as I remembered the first time he had got up from his seat because I was leaving the dining table. It was a type of half stand, half crouch position he had adopted, leaning on the table with two large hands. I thought he was going to break wind and told him so.

We laughed a lot. My laughter was gut-wrenching and linked somehow to the sex organs. I flirted for England, my subconscious acknowledging that I wanted to touch this man emotionally and physically. That first evening together ended abruptly with a kiss on both cheeks. I saw him the next day. We walked towards each other through the crowds in the Palais, making eye contact all the way until we were close enough to touch. I was in awe of him, and drowned my feelings of desire in stilted waves of business conversation.

'It was a lovely evening Diana,' he'd said, looking so tired I wanted to hug him there and then right on the spot.

'Yes, wasn't it,' I replied quietly. 'Anyway, I wondered if you could give me some information on the children's television programmes you mentioned.'

He had looked surprised that I was reducing a potentially intimate conversation to business.

'Yes of course,' he rallied. My hand shook slightly as I handed him my business card.

'Let's speak on the phone soon,' he said.

I nodded in agreement and tore myself away. Cursing his living in New York, blotting out the sight of the Russian three gold rings on the fourth finger of his left hand. But consoling myself with thoughts of our future

11

there together. Even at that early stage I'd have followed him over to the Big Apple like a shot if he'd asked.

Our relationship, if that's what it could be called, was not consummated for another year. Much of the foreplay was via telephone, a twisting of phone wires, a heart-hammering jolt every time it rang outside normal hours. A more than satisfactory conclusion had been reached in Cannes at my second MIP market. The revelation that making love could be so much more than mere sex concluded with the inevitable parting talk about the future and the shocking, miserable, truth of it. No children, but definitely taken. There followed a year of soul searching to acknowledge this cold fact whilst his pursuit continued. I was still clinging to the notion that Max was ideal for me, ignoring the guilt that our affair was causing. Now in year three I finally knew. He wasn't the handsome commitment-phobe who'd finally found the woman of his dreams, I told myself over and over, but a cheater, playing away from home. But the pulsing physical excitement I was feeling now a couple of months since our last "encounter" meant the anticipation of seeing him again wasn't something I could deny to anybody, least of all myself.

I took the steps up to my room three at a time and flung myself into the shower, dried myself, carefully applied make-up and dressed in a pale orange jacket and blue linen trousers. Ten minutes later I was walking into the Palais and, after a bit of crowd searching, found Sarah.

We ran through our schedule for the day: eight meetings, including pitching for two new clients. Our work involved sprinting between exhibition stands, organising, cajoling and interviewing American, English, French and Canadian television clients. It was a delicate balance between taking information about their programmes, business deals and events they felt important, and then disseminating the data into journalistic intelligence. This would be printed, relayed on radio reports or even broadcast in the various documentaries being produced that year about the business of international television.

'First meeting Leworthy & Price on the Primetime stand,' Sarah announced, straightening a silver brooch attached to the lapel of her well-cut jacket. 'I bumped into them last night and they want journos and photographers on the stand at 3pm this afternoon. Something about a deal with NHK in Japan.'

Primetime were then the biggest distributor of television programmes in the UK.

We raced for the escalators. The four-storey building heaved with over 8,000 people from 150 countries, all charged with the energy of those who have people to see, places to go. We joined the crowds and weaved and dodged our way up three floors to the press room, past hundreds of stands blaring out their wares in technicolour vision. Indian, Spanish and Hungarian companies made up most of the third floor: mini-cultures blasting out from banks of television screens, a blaze of noise and colour, a techno Turkish bazaar.

Experienced industry veteran that I was, I knew how to stagger energy levels through the five-day periods that the markets spanned. That day we had a further pitch lunch with a broadcaster and dinner with a party of journalists, organised by us to market our company.

I had met Sarah when we worked together on a magazine called *TV World*. It was run by a small London publishing firm which produced an unusual combination of titles in far-flung places including the Far East, Africa and Russia. The publisher was a canny man called Derek who had a naughty grin and a business mind that closed like a trap if you suggested a pay rise. He was, however, eternally generous with his travel budgets and within weeks of joining as Deputy Editor, I was travelling to places I had previously only dreamed about – New York, Los Angeles, Monte Carlo, Houston and Cannes.

Christine and Jane joined us on the press room balcony, clasping notebooks close to their chests, Jane with a biro behind her left ear.

'We need stories already,' Jane giggled. 'Tony wants news exclusives and he wants them NOW!'

They were working for the Exhibition organisers, MIDEM, producers of the daily papers for the television market. I had worked on two markets as a journalist and knew the pressures all too well. We stood beside the railings of the balcony. Whilst the others nattered and looked down across the vast sweep of the exhibition floor, I studied the appointment list Sarah and I had completed.

'There's this possible new astrology series with Joan Collins and Omar Shariff.' They both looked at me, straining towards my notes, two journos sniffing out a good story.

'I haven't mentioned it before,' I explained. 'We just don't know if it's a goer. There's been some problems with budgets and the backers are proving a bit too mysterious.'

'I don't care,' interjected Christine, producing a biro from behind her notebook. 'Fire away. If I have to do just one more story on the size of US programming exports I swear I'm going to drop my drawers in front of the French Minister for Culture.'

'Speaking of large US exports,' hissed Jane. 'Eyes right.'

My heart lurched. Max was walking towards us, smiling. By the time he reached the balcony, my tactful colleagues had slipped away, muttering excuses about deadlines and broken phones. Sarah whispered details of where we should meet later. I barely heard her, the blood was thumping in my ears.

'Good morning Diana,' drawled Max. Adding quietly, 'You look beautiful.'

I forced myself to look into his pale blue eyes and pulled myself up to my full 5ft 10 inch height. I breathed slowly, recalling a promise I had made to myself: to keep cool, to appear less interested.

'Morning Max. Thank you. You look well.'

He kissed me on both cheeks.

'I came to look for you. To congratulate you on your new business venture. I've heard it's going well. Perhaps you could do something for me.' He grinned and gently fondled the fine gold chain I was wearing around my neck. I stood still and let him. He had given it to me.

I felt lost, I could feel my previous resolution melting away.

'We should talk,' I said. 'And not about business, although I would be delighted to handle your press and publicity.' I smiled and attempted to look directly into his eyes. He looked faintly saddened and nodded in agreement. The sun was shining on his hair.

'Are you going to the CBC party?' I asked.

He shook his head slowly.

Just as well, I told myself as my heart sank.

'Can you get me a ticket?'

My stomach tightened in anticipation of seeing him at an interesting event, late at night. 'Yes, I…'

'Majestic bar, 10.30 tonight?' he suggested, backing away slowly, his eyes penetrating deep into mine.

I hurried down three sets of escalators, feeling ashamed at the renewed vigour in my step. I smiled at people I didn't know and yelled greetings at those I did. I both cursed and loved the fact that Max could have this regenerative effect on me.

The air in the ground floor of the Palais was static with the electricity of thousands of television sets and video recorders pumping their contents and a cacophony of sound into the enclosed atmosphere.

I made my way to the stand of Rissos, the Greek producer who was trying to raise funds for the astrology TV show.

'You ask the computer a single question, mentally in your head,' he wasted no time ushering me towards the seat in front of his elaborate, costly PC astrology system. 'It will give you a 12 page tarot spread. All it needs is your place and time of birth.'

'16 October 1960, 8.15pm, the Wirral, West Kirby. Quick birth, mother knackered, father delighted. Second child, first daughter.'

I was eager to see my future. My love life was in a bit of turmoil. In a way Max was the least of my problems. He was the love of my life, yes, and, romantic though I am, I had also resigned myself to the hopelessness of the situation long before this trip. For, by now, I had grown a complicated multidimensional love life all of my own.

I was still living with Duncan in a together but not together situation. We'd grown apart but shared a mortgage on a flat in Bromley and weren't entirely sure what we were going to do about it. Whilst Duncan slept in the spare room and lived his busy life as a chef in a central London restaurant, "fake" dating the occasional girl, I was a young woman desperately seeking chemistry with a new man, anyone to pull me away from the electric glue that kept me sticking to Max. I was therefore an ideal candidate for a touch of astro-driven psycho-babble.

Rissos plotted the coordinates on a cheaply printed chart and nodded at me to ask my mental question. 'Easy,' my brain ticked over. 'Will I marry Max?'

I hated hearing myself say that. I'd started thinking as much about his wife as I did about him. I felt for her, *she* deserved him and *I* didn't. That was the simple truth of it.

My palms felt a bit sticky and my heartbeat rose slightly in preparation. 'All a load of nonsense,' I said to myself. 'All to be taken lightly, with a pinch of salt.'

With Rissos distracted by a new visitor to his stand, I snatched at the pages as the computer spat them out, glad to be able to scan the words in privacy. Nine cards had been drawn and each had a page of information. Most of it was, as I had predicted, written in the standard and frequently ambiguous horoscopic language. The answer to my mental question was evident from page one. Even a piece of American hardware referred to my current romance with the words "infatuation", "gullibility" and "instability". It went on to forecast into the future year ahead so I read on, in search of better news.

The summer was going to be interesting. The World card had been drawn. I knew this was a fantastic card to receive. I smiled and then panicked as I read through the whole page. A shiver crept up the back of my neck and into my brain. It *was* the World card, only reversed. My eyes leaped to the "Key reversed meaning" section at the bottom of the page.

"Overbearing restrictions, irreversibility, danger!"

And worse, the computer print-out had defaulted.

It had cut off part of the page.

'Well Diana,' said Rissos turning back to me as his visitor left. 'Wealth and riches beyond your wildest dreams? Ha ha ha.'

'It's a load of bollocks, Rissos.' I stood up and shoved the stack of computer papers into a nearby bin.

CHAPTER THREE

Guilty

The catering trolley trundled slowly towards me, steered by a beaming, over-friendly hostess who stopped and chatted with every passenger.

It was 11 in the morning, but I didn't think twice about accepting the second mini-bottle of vodka offered with my can of Schweppes and pack of peanuts. I was no alcoholic but the rules of normal life didn't hold sway in international airspace. I was anxious to lap up all of the unreality left to me before my normal life with all of its problems intervened at touchdown. I tapped my foot impatiently. The flight time from Cannes to London was only an hour and fifty minutes.

At last she parked up next to me.

'Good trip then?' she beamed, filling my glass brimful with ice and picking out a slice of lemon. Air travel was like that then, glamorous, generous and friendly.

'Yes, brilliant,' I grinned right back at her. She wasn't to know that the second bottle was more for drowning my sorrows over Max and that stupid astrology reading than celebrating our achievements, great as they were. We'd done it, though. Sarah and I had pulled off setting up a business that was now an established player on the world stage of television. I'd not only perfected the Cannes Stare, this year, which involved keeping an interest in the person you are talking to whilst being acutely aware of what's happening all around you; but had set up meetings for possible deals with some of the biggest names on the planet, including a forthcoming meeting in London with the head honcho of Brazil's *TV Globo* no less. MediaVision was cooking. The mess of my love life aside, the future looked bright indeed.

Though I knew that whatever Max and I had shared had been fuelled by the unstoppable all-too-real life force of love and lust, I didn't believe in the tarot. I felt astrology could be a general indicator for personality traits and had used the skills adopted from Linda Goodman's *Sun Signs* books to great effect as a dinner party piece. Everything else was a combination of psychology and pure hocus pocus. How could it be anything else? Rissos had obviously invested a fortune in his stupid machine along with its glossy brochure with its word-perfect PR blurb. Yes, I'd been gullible for a weak moment, but had quickly seen through his pitch to the precarious nature of the project. It wasn't something I'd be pushing.

Just a little longer. I sipped at my vodka & tonic and looked down at the clouds, letting myself wallow in memories of the most beautiful, perfect lover I'd left behind and was determined to never see again. This was Max's world, up in the sunshine and the clouds where service came with a smile and rules were only there to be broken.

He'd seemed like the final and crucial piece in the jigsaw of my life. But it had turned out to be twisted and warped, a piece that distorted the whole picture. I'd fallen in love, he filled my head and influenced my thoughts. He had fallen in love with me but he loved his wife and would not be leaving her, which made him, in my moral mind, a good man.

A close friend, Dinah, had shaken her head when I'd explained how I felt about him. She was good on emotional theories. 'Married men tend to leave their wives within three months of starting an affair. Or not at all.'

I'd dressed with Game On intent for the CBC party that night. Short black velvet skirt, emerald green top and silver jewellery. Hair up, earrings on. Perfume sprayed discreetly. Lashings of body lotion. Sheer black stockings. New garter belt. 2 inch heels. Six feet tall.

'Try messing with that Max,' I'd said to the reflection in the mirror.

We met at The Hotel Majestic, a magnificent crisp white stucco building on the Croisette, with lush green palm trees dotted in the gardens by the pool. The air was heavy with business discussion. Business couldn't have been further from my mind, not that sort anyway.

Annoyingly I was first. I thought about walking around the block but decided against it. I ordered a sparkling water and forced myself to remember the image from the year before. An image of Max standing in the distance, a large glossy carrier bag in one hand, the other hand waving almost dismissively to me. He was waving goodbye, returning to America after we'd spent two nights together, making a love which had made me the "other woman". A position I'd come to despise and would not countenance. The carrier bag contained expensive boutique clothes for his wife.

Whilst I'd felt sick with fear and an infatuated love, Max was able to put distance between us – both in miles and emotionally. I'd coped by launching into fantasy bordering on obsession. It wasn't going to work. I'd set myself up for heartache and it was coming on fast. I didn't want this type of life. Seeking out heightened pleasure in hotel rooms, a source of deceit, places where people stayed on the way to their real lives.

I was determined to say what I had to say. To state my reasons for finishing it clearly and sensibly. To rest my case and put an end to this torture.

I knew when he'd walked into the building before I saw him because my stomach had done its involuntary leap into my throat. By the time he sank into the red velvet seat next to me my whole body was pulsing. The world-weary waiter swept the dirty ashtray off the table with disdain.

With heart hammering in my ribcage, I crossed my legs and lit a cigarette.

'Go on, say it. Speak,' said a voice from within but my mouth remained closed.

'I may have some business in Paris next month,' he fiddled with a cufflink. His head moved nearer to mine and I instinctively moved towards him.

'Perhaps MediaVision could have some more French work to do?'

'No I don't think so.'

He jerked his head back in surprise.

'I can't,' I whispered. 'I don't think this is doing me a lot of good.' I could barely breathe and grabbed my glass off the table, drinking as quickly and noiselessly as I could. Max sipped his drink, eyeing me narrowly over the rim of his glass. He looked disappointed. A facial expression I had seen on him before when I'd previously tried to stop the alchemy between us.

'I'm 29 and our relationship, or situation, isn't doing me much good. And you're a nice man, Max, a good man really. You feel guilty and so do I.'

'I'm weak, certainly, yes, and I do feel guilty but it's convenient, it works.'

'CONVENIENT?' I yelped and shut my mouth quickly. Other heads in the bar had looked up.

'I'm fed up with secrecy,' I hissed. 'And I'm fed up of being 29 with no prospect of having children with the man I lo – er, someone I want to be with. A man who is married to someone else and who shows no sign of leaving. Not that I have ever asked you to. I just thought you might…' my voice trailed off.

'You mention children a lot, Diana,' he responded, with not a hint of kindness in his voice.

'It's not on your agenda I know. You've made it very clear that you never want children. You work in children's television programming and you don't even seem to like them!'

No doubt recognising an alley of conversation he did not wish to go down, he changed the subject, slightly.

'We shouldn't do this, but I thought you could handle it. You seem so strong.' He took hold of my hand and caressed my fingertips. 'I love to be with you Diana, but I have responsibilities.'

'I can handle it. Or perhaps I can't. I don't know,' my words faltered away. Tears were close now, pooling dangerously at the back of my throat. I had to be in control to do this. I cleared my voice, gulping back the taste of the fizzy drink and cigarettes.

'It hasn't been convenient for me, Max. My relationship with Duncan is ruined. You want to leave your wife at certain times of the year and come to me. I would be living for seeing you and that would be crazy. It can't go on.'

I wrestled with my hands as if they were the enemies.

'We'd better leave,' I sniffed. 'You can walk me back to the hotel.'

'What about the CBC party? You're dressed for it.' He looked me up and down in that way.

'I've changed my mind. I've got you a ticket but I don't want to go. You have it if you want.'

He looked strained and I thought good because he wasn't going to cry like I was when I left for home.

We stepped out into the magic of an evening in Cannes. The sea breeze teased gently at my hair, blowing it across my eyes. The lights on the Croisette lit up the velvet balm of the night. Our feet, walking in unison, were the only sound to punctuate the stillness. I felt miserable at what could have been.

We stopped abruptly outside my hotel. The last steps of our walk had been made in silence and had gone too quickly.

He slid his arms around my back inside my jacket and rested his head gently on my shoulder. He moved his hands down onto my bottom and began stroking in small delicate circles. Our mouths met and, resistance fading, my lower abdomen trembled. The pungent aroma of yellow mimosa was all around us.

'No!' I broke away and held him at arms' length.

'No,' I said again loudly and looked into his eyes. He was smiling, thinking that this was a new dimension to our complex games. He was thinking he could win me over. I stepped backwards and well away from him. I swung open the heavy glass door and looked back. Tension and desire swirled. As usual an evening was going to end with more unanswered questions. I knew Max would keep trying and he knew the bonds were not yet broken. He looked at me. I stood inside and looked back again. With one hand on my hip I raised the other and slowly made a beckoning motion.

I am human and female, I told myself, crunching on an ice-cube and wishing that the flight would last forever. Wishing that, reversed World card or not, I wouldn't have to face the problems which waited for me at home.

I'd be walking straight into it: Duncan would be at the flat, hoping I'd go back to him.

My situation with Max had put the final nail into my relationship with Duncan. We'd been living together for five years. Engaged for three. It was right for him but hadn't been right for me for a number of years. Maybe it wasn't fair to blame Max completely. We would have finished anyway. Our paths had diverged when I started to run my own business, with all the travelling that involved. Duncan was a chef and, as his girlfriend, I'd been left to my own devices every evening. Then the situation reversed and I was the one to take flight, literally. Meeting Max had set Duncan's and my future together in stone, at the bottom of a very deep lake.

We slept in separate rooms. Even though you couldn't dissolve a mortgage overnight any more than you could dissolve a marriage overnight, I was, cruelly, holding onto him at a distance, just in case.

But although Duncan and I had lost our way I still didn't want to hurt him. I despised myself sometimes for not making a clean cut. It was as if I was hedging my bets. Waiting for someone else to turn up whilst Duncan waited patiently for me to realise that no one would love me as much as he did.

CHAPTER FOUR

Born To Run

'Good trip?' Duncan greeted me in habitual cheerful mode, his mop of curly brown hair bouncing atop his cute face.

I assuaged a slight guilt pang by placing a bottle of duty free Jack Daniels on the glass-topped coffee table in front of us.

We'd bought the table and many other pieces of furniture together. As a couple we had fallen into a mortgage trap when financial realities displaced any rational thoughts of living together forever. Shunted from one rental rip-off to another, I'd stalked off to affordable Bromley and fallen for our flat because it overlooked a cricket pitch and the then owners looked content and happy in their sweat tops and baggy pants. We soon realised that sportswear was a prerequisite to living where we did. Life was easier four floors up if you chose to run up all 120 steps. The effort was always worth it. The flat had atmosphere with attic rooms under the eaves and stunning panoramas of the Kent countryside.

Duncan and I had remained friends through our protracted break-up but commuting into London for work was a drag and I was looking for a way out. I frequently pondered on where Duncan and I had gone wrong and came to the conclusion that suspicion, the death-knell of most relationships, had set in early on. Insecure in his love for me, Duncan had been at times a ferocious flirt. He adored the company of women, which I didn't mind. What I did take offence at was his ability to suggest that he could "have" any of my single girlfriends, unless I showed him the love he felt he deserved. The doubts had nibbled into my mind early in the relationship and had become roaring big bites by the time we split. However, we looked after each other. We were caught in a modern situation, forced to think of finance first, which, thankfully, had bought us a flat with two bedrooms. Friendship came second and love, well, I had initiated the split, so I relegated myself to the box room.

The next morning I kick-started my over-indulged body from Cannes with an aerobics session at the local gym with Becky, a well-heeled cockney girlfriend who lived with her boyfriend Gordon in the flat below us. Becky, tall and slim, bordering on skinny, but laying an eternal claim on fat, would pinch herself for proof, saying, 'Look Di, how's that for half an inch?'

We had a ritualistic system for the gym, standing at the front of the class, staring at our "fat" figures in the ceiling to floor mirrors, analysing which bits had to come off. The fact that we didn't mind staring at ourselves probably meant the thrice-weekly torture was working its magic.

We discussed relationships in intense detail, as I did with all of my girlfriends, offering non-judgmental advice when I could and listening intently to their thoughts on my own emotional dilemmas.

Afterwards we panted our way through a cold shower and then skipped into the hot sauna, breathing in the nostril-curling heat.

'This'll have ter be me last sauna Di,' muffled Becky through the rising steam hissing its way up from the searing coals.

'Why's that Becks?'

'I'm pregnant.'

I felt a stab of envy. My biological clock had commenced its ticking at about the same time as I'd met Max but I'd smothered it, keeping work as my priority.

'Oh Becks, that's fantastic.' I reached through the billowing steams to cuddle her. She was wet and slippery.

Sarah and I were due to discuss insurances for the company with our accountant later in the week and we'd both agreed that, if it were possible, we'd take a policy out on one of us getting pregnant, rather than life insurance for the other business partner.

Refreshed and fully charged, I made the commute into London. It was a pleasure to gaze through the train's dirty windows out to the spring day, the type of day when you notice some of the beauties of London architecture. It was Saturday but as owner of my own company I had the responsibility of progressing the momentum created by the successful start in Cannes. Making my way to Primetime's offices in the West End, I hummed a George Michael tune captured in my head from listening to my Sony Walkman. I buzzed the bell and waited for an answer.

'Ullo.'

'Hello it's Diana Hill, MediaVision.'

The door clicked open and my heels click clacked across the marble floored foyer to the lift. In an energetic spurt I ignored the lift's welcoming opening and decided to dash up the three floors to Primetimes's offices.

Expecting to see someone I knew from the company, I was more than surprised at the vision before me.

He nodded and offered his hand, 'Andrew. I do computers.'

'Gosh,' I wanted to say. 'With those navy blue eyes, and shiny black hair, I'd quite like to do you!' But instead I smiled and said I'd come to work on a Japanese television project on Primetime's sophisticated computer set-up.

Funnily enough, almost as soon as I settled down to my work I found I was having enormous problems in operating the complicated computer systems. Something that hadn't troubled me before. He pulled up a swivel chair.

We both watched the computer screen with me fingering the mouse and Andrew pointing out keys to work the new database correctly. He sat close to me. I could smell soap, cigarettes and oil.

Throughout the day we made each other vats of coffee, treacle black for him and blobs of powdered milk for me. I gently moved the conversation from mice, bytes and other computer jargon to office jokes, jostling our words finally to the personal – and relationships. I'd already discovered he was originally from Derbyshire, hence his northern accent, that he had a motorbike (a BMW500cc) and while he liked to ask the odd question, what he really wanted to do was talk about himself. He had a slight edginess that made me think he had a lot to reveal.

'Are you courting?' he asked suddenly. I half spluttered a mouthful of coffee.

'What an old-fashioned phrase!' Then I saw a flash of hurt register in his eyes. 'It's sweet though,' I added quickly. 'And no, I'm not.'

He grinned mischievously revealing a set of perfect white teeth.

'I had my fingers burnt recently. And what about you?' I asked in my best Summerzet accent. 'Be you courting my dearie?'

'Nah, recently finished.' He swept the mop of black fringe from his forehead and bit a fingernail thoughtfully as if he was wondering whether he should reveal any more. 'Should've been getting married today.'

'What?' I snapped, a decibel above deaf level, just the dreaded mention of the M word making my hackles rise.

He didn't notice and began his own soliloquy.

'She'd bought the dress and everything. Cancelled five weeks ago. Witch. Pete says I'm better off without her. I went Motocross riding while she bought the dress. We'd been living together for five years. Didn't have a clue. She was probably seeing someone else.'

'What was her name?' I purposely used the past tense – always best for people who should be mentally buried.

'Janine.'

I tut-tutted and shook my head in sympathetic sorrow, thinking, more fool you Janine, why did you let this one go?

'Come on,' I said. 'We both deserve a drink.' Switching off the computers, we headed for a local pub. I didn't notice at first, I was too busy concentrating on looking animated at what Andrew was saying, but he seemed to open the whole of his throat to drink.

Six Pils lagers with little wodges of lime on top and more than eight pints of bitter later we staggered out of the pub into the central London night, catching a drift of sweet Spring air.

'Will you be in next week?' he asked, swaying slightly.

'Of course,' I smiled. My veins awash with alcohol, I couldn't stop grinning to myself all the way home, fantasising about kissing Andrew on Primetime's conference desk.

It took two weeks of cut and thrust flirting to secure a first snog with Andrew. He was deeply hurt by Janine and I had to be extremely discreet so that the client wouldn't suss that I was making a beeline for their computer boffin. I took a great deal of interest in the Japanese project.

'This mouse is in need of a damned good servicing,' I would whisper at Sarah in the Primetime board meetings on PR strategy. 'And I know which hard drive would do the job.' She'd already guessed from our body language that our intentions went beyond the presentation of a detailed television project.

We'd sneak out to the local pub at lunchtime and sit, thighs together, in the snug room upstairs. I'm not too bright with lunchtime drinks but, with purpose in mind, valiantly sipped at spritzers while Andrew throated a couple of pints. One lunchtime, as we went to split off again at the door of the pub, he suddenly placed his hands around my face and kissed me full on the mouth, gently worming his tongue in for a little search. We clung together, suspended in time, probably looking like a tacky couple from a Paris postcard. Unbeknown to us, our little session was spotted by other members of the Primetime team.

The kissing established stage two on the rocket pad of the relationship. Stage one had been a great deal of talking and a hair-matting motorbike ride the previous weekend, Andrew's own version of foreplay. I skittishly donned the heavy crash helmet, thinking, bollocks, this is going to smear my make-up. We set off. He broke two promises in less than five minutes. One: not to go fast. Two: not to go out of London. A gentle cruise quickly became a dispatch rider's dream as he chased green lights and ignored the beating I was giving him on his back. He then pointed stiffly with a leathered glove at the sign for Brighton. I clocked his twinkling eyes through our visors, squeezed my arms right around his body and leant my head on his broad shoulders. I closed my eyes and he opened his throttle wide.

Brighton was wonderful. We fell over in the sea, went on funfair rides and ate hotdogs.

Andrew still spoke of his past, his baggage, of Janine, so much at times that we could have put her in a suitcase and swung it from around his neck. I wooed and cooed, trying to adopt patience, a virtue I had little patience for. But I was secure in the knowledge that there was no point in trying to push for a relationship if he was still obsessed with the woman who'd practically dropped him at the altar on her way to another life.

I'd noticed a few irritating habits in my new amour. A propensity for taking a fiver at a time from the hole in the wall cash machine; a desire to speak openly and freely about his own recent heartache, but with no reciprocal need to hear anything of my past life, and he would sometimes eat and drink so quickly that I was afraid his lovemaking might have the same characteristics. Still, these slight anomalies were easily dispatched from the mind in the wake of true lust. He had many endearing qualities, a delicious sensuality, especially when it came to kissing, an amusing sense of humour speckled with funny phrases, he was devastatingly handsome and he loved his mum.

As to his irritating habit of eating too quickly, it couldn't be compared to his love-making as I found out some six weeks after meeting him.

Life turns up its usual surprises however. One evening we were in a pub near to where Andrew lived in Leytonstone and I found myself mentally pleading to be put out of my non-sex misery. I'd first met his friends a few weeks earlier – John, who worked in the city, and his earnest girlfriend Susan; and Pete, or Mr Plod because he worked for the police force. The June night was warm and a low sun threw out a glow as we sat in the beer garden on wooden seats, taking it in turns to buy drinks from the bar.

Andrew was talking computers with John, his free hand – the one without the pint in it, softly stroking the skin on top of my foot, making me inwardly squirm with pleasure.

We were planning a motorbike trip to Belgium. I imagined beautiful walks alongside the river in Bruges, afternoons of rampant passion with the sunlight streaming through fifteenth century windows, and candlelit dinners. The men, in between spreadsheet discussions and ram sized equations, interrupted my thoughts with the reality – chips and mayonnaise, camping in a tent and watching the Motocross, the principal reason for going.

'It's the dog's bollocks Di,' exclaimed Andrew, his eyes going all dreamy. I smiled my Mona Lisa smile in response. Pleased that I was part of Andrew's team. Delighted that I had obviously made a hit with his fairly reserved friends and trying to stop imagining what a baby made between Andrew and I would look like.

Mr Plod walked in and announced a lightning underground strike. I panicked. Leytonstone was the back of beyond for me to get home from without tube transport.

'You can stay the night at mine,' Andrew declared. 'I'll sleep on the floor.'

'Oh aye,' said Ploddy, eyeing up my reaction.

I thought about a cab, but as much as MediaVision was doing well, cab fares of nearly £80 (around $118) would not look good running through the expenses sheets. I plumped for a further Pils lager to drown my indecision.

A couple of hours later Andrew and I were snogging passionately in his tiny lounge. It seemed my normal "wait for three month rule" was to be broken. The overhead light blazed and the curtains weren't closed. To prevent a little show for any net-twitching neighbours we side shuffled to his bedroom and tumbled into the unmade bed.

'Aren't you forgetting something?' I whispered as we grappled under a duvet that hadn't seen washing powder the better side of a month.

'A raincoat,' I added coyly. He looked puzzled. Was I suggesting some fetish?

'Oh yeah, of course,' and he scrambled in his wallet for the Durex.

His packet of three disappeared that night.

The next morning I made breakfast and lunch and tidied up the small ground floor flat. We took a bike ride to an old church and wandered hand in hand around the fields. We returned for more sex and then lay in the garden until it was time for a barbecue. I stayed again Saturday night but left the next day, aware of putting on a show of continued independence – I wanted him to think I had another life.

Andrew took me back to Bromley on the motorbike. I had a lot of work to do. Sarah and her boyfriend Justin were getting married and she'd been busy with all the arrangements. I needed to write a good proposal for a major TV company based in Latin America. Their forte was telenovela movies and soaps – Mills and Boon with a Spanish accent. My nights of passion with Andrew had given me plenty of inspiration. But first I had to look to Duncan, who was displaying distinct signs of distress at my overnight absences.

I'd already told him about Andrew and my waltzing in on Sunday morning whistling *This Hill is Alive With The Sound of Music* was a clear hint that I had experienced the type of weekend Duncan and I had enjoyed in the past. It proved too much and his sweet face crumpled. I felt immediately guilty, but what could I do? Duncan and I hadn't slept together for over two years, yet neither of us had had the courage to knock the whole thing on the head. We were like brother and sister, but I knew that Duncan was secretly harbouring thoughts of us getting back together again. The last thing I wanted to do was to hurt him. So I talked endlessly to him that day, and tried my utmost to make him feel better about an extremely awkward predicament. He revived but still wore the face of a person in sadness. The face I'd worn in my experiences with Max. You believe you've found the right one, they just can't see it yet.

Sarah waved us off on our journey to Belgium. I couldn't quite believe that I'd agreed to go, and I looked back at her pensive face thinking, what if we have an accident? I had no leathers and my trust in Andrew had to be absolute. He proved to be a good, steady driver over long distances and only kicked the bike into full speed on good motorways. The thrill of feeling the wind in my face and of seeing the countryside changing in the June heat was immeasurable, producing a genuine feeling of freedom.

It was late evening by the time we got to Bruges, via ferry from Dover. I asked Andrew where he'd booked us in for the night. His sheepish "naughty boy" grin was the only response.

'Where are we going to sleep?' I demanded, acting like a typical Libran, desirous of all things comfortable. Warm baths, luxury bed. Continental breakfasts.

'We'll find somewhere, don't worry.'

We didn't. There was a festival on as well as the Motocross. Like the proverbial Joseph and Mary there was no room for us at any inn.

I drank myself into a near stupor. I wore a mantle of vexation and fumed silently, acknowledging that this was our first row. Andrew's attempt at apology came in the form of introducing me to black, bitter Belgium beers. I chucked them down.

We slept in a field, illegally. So toxic was my hangover the next day that I stung my bare bottom on nettles trying to squat and pee. I cursed Andrew and while we watched Motocross perched on a vertical mud bank, a hornet sniffed out my anger and aimed for my arm. The sting brought tears to my eyes and a howl from my throat. Andrew rushed me down the treacherous slopes towards the first aid tents. The uniformed first-aiders were highly amused. At the least they expected some broken bones, all they saw was a nasty sting and they sent me off with a smear of Savlon and a patronising chuckle.

Andrew implied I was being a baby and that really made my blood boil. I restrained my anger but while he slept that afternoon on a grassy bank, I booked us into an expensive business hotel, out of the price range of the tourists.

Luxury restored! After hot showers and a quick shag we enjoyed an evening aimlessly roaming on the town. Like a contestant on the TV dating show *Take Me Out* I was determined to enjoy myself. But Andrew could be dogged and stubborn, and sometimes displayed a selfish desire for his own pastimes – computing, Motocross and beer   which made me feel that I was only ever tagging along for the sexual ride. He was bringing out my moody self – and a perniciously moody self I could be, although on the whole I was nearly always optimistic and tried to be kind whenever possible. Not that I expected us to be perfect, just that the effort seemed a bit one-sided at times.

Belgium established the distance in our relationship. I knew that if I was made up of, say, seven complex layers, with spirituality at the centre, Andrew was only ever going to scratch the surface. He wasn't a curious person. But he seemed quite happy most of the time and I was willing to go along for the journey together.

At 29 I was facing the dilemma that many career women face. We were introduced to an exciting new world of independence, our eyes opened by liberation to strive for something for ourselves. It wasn't barefoot in the kitchen, more like high heels in the boardroom, but this financial and work-related independence had raised our aspirations. We wanted more and expected more from partners. And those partners were difficult to find.

I felt immense relief that the curse of the married man was finally behind me. I was in charge of my own life and old enough to know that perfection didn't exist. My biological clock ticked away, hormonally treacherous to my ambition.

CHAPTER FIVE

Nessun Dorma

Andrew and I fell into a pattern of affiliation with no momentum towards commitment. We'd see each other a couple of times during the week and fairly consistently at weekends. One weekend I decided to break the pattern and went off without him to see my parents in Cheshire. They lived in a stunning apartment in the grounds of a country estate, complete with mansion house owned, and lived in, for 800 years, by the lords of the land. The buildings are surrounded by endless rolling fields of green pretty countryside and the grounds of the estate include marked out walks through a forest and over bridges that rainbow arch a lazy stream.

I travelled up to Cheshire with my business partner Sarah and her husband Justin who were going to stay with friends. They dropped me off at a nearby village and I waited in the hot sun for Mum to collect me. I couldn't wait to see her. For years we'd established a deep friendship that meant we could talk as mates. I would give her most of the gen on Andrew and listen to her wise advice. Dad, a businessman all his working life, was company secretary of MediaVision. His ambition filtered down through the genes to me and he would be pleased with the way it was going. They had together enjoyed a glorious summer so far, appreciating the company of their pleasant neighbours, when they weren't enthralled with the footie World Cup, revelling in the TV soundtrack to that sporting event – *Nessun Dorma*.

I sat astride a stone wall, swinging my legs and nodding my head, singing along quietly with the sounds of *Tears for Fears* and *Sade* from the Sony stuck to my head. Time passed slowly and, growing weary of people watching, I began to feel slightly anxious. Mum was never late.

An hour past our rendezvous time my forehead had become wet with sweat and burnt from the afternoon sunshine. Sometimes it's hard to remember what it was like before mobile phones arrived. I leapt with relief when I saw her suddenly appear and walk towards me. But something was wrong, she wasn't smiling and her head hung low. She was looking at her feet.

'Your dad's had an accident. He tripped over first thing this morning and won't call the doctor. I think he needs a doctor.'

We walked quickly to the car and Mum drove in silence, distracted with panic-stricken thoughts.

Dad was lying on his bed, a cut slashed deep above his left eye and across his forehead. He grimaced weakly at me.

'Now then Dad, why no doctor?'

'Don't need a Doctor sweetie, I'll be alright in a minute.'

'It happened at 7 o'clock this morning,' said Mum, hovering at the door. I sat on the bed and studied him.

'That's a nasty cut,' I said as I took his hand. My heart jumped as I realised half his body was shaking involuntarily.

'What about this movement, this shaking, Dad?' I said, trying to smooth the quivery muscles with the palm of my hand.

'Don't know, can't make it stop. Do you think I need a doctor?'

'That cut needs stitches Dad.' I looked at Mum who left for the telephone.

An hour later an ambulance arrived to take Dad to Macclesfield hospital. Two men had to chair lift him down the stairs. I went with him in the ambulance, listening to the calming patter of one of the men.

'Now then, nothing to worry about.'

'But I can't feel my leg. Or my arm. Will I be alright?'

'Sure. Don't think about it. We'll get you sorted.'

At the hospital while they stitched the cut, Dad moaned quietly. As usual he was refusing all anaesthetics. He is the only man I know to have had his teeth drilled with no Novocaine, using the excuse, "I can't stand to feel numb for hours later". I headed for the smoking room, not for a cigarette, I was giving up, but for a cry. A nurse came in behind me and asked about family history. 'We think your father's had a stroke,' she explained while I wept without sound.

'I've not had a stroke sweetie. Come on, take me home. I'm not staying here.'

Dad, newly bandaged was going against medical orders and refusing to stay the night. I had the peculiar task of pushing him in a wheelchair and felt all his power, his energy and his health falling away as he was reduced to being pushed in a seat with two large wheels.

Early evening saw Mum and I struggling to lift him from the car and back into the house. By evening the right side of his body was totally paralysed.

The doctor phoned the next day with the shocking announcement that the following 24 hours were going to be crucial. His delivery of the words seemed callous, even cold, the profession disliking patients who discharge themselves from hospital. 'There is a high probability that your father will die.' Conjuring up every prayer I could, I left Mum trying again to cajole Dad back into a different hospital, and flung myself to my knees.

'Please, please,' I whispered aloud. 'Do anything.' I clasped my hands together. 'Take anything from me, but don't let my daddy die. Take Andrew from me,' I went on, now fervently holding my hands up in the direction of the ceiling. 'Don't let him die.'

Dad didn't die. As he'd correctly diagnosed, he hadn't had a stroke. Two days later a wise White Coat from Manchester Royal Infirmary suggested that he was suffering from a nerve paralysis caused by him smashing his head on the window sash when he fell. He'd fractured his neck and had been within millimetres of either total paralysis or death. Gradually the severe immobility waned and, due to his incredible strength of mind over matter, he was walking again. Albeit slowly and with a slight limp.

I had to return to London to work. Andrew picked me up from the train station. He smiled his broadest and I flung myself into his arms. He was also extremely close to his parents. Although they lived in Germany, his father was a child psychiatrist on an army base. He tried to see them as much as he could. My respect for him grew. An empathy became incorporated into our relationship and that night he held me, stroking my head as a father would his child.

It was in that moment, I think, that I felt a release from Max. I really was moving on. It was all slowly slowly catchie the worm with Andrew, but this new empathy in him had surprised and delighted me. The only real problem on the horizon was to sort out the practicalities. To make the final break with Duncan.

My dad's accident was a powerful trigger. I now knew more than ever that I wanted to settle down and have a child. And, miracles of miracles, I'd found the man to do it with. I was ready to put Max behind me, sort it out with Duncan, and go for it with Andrew.

There followed a few blissful weeks with Andrew, and increasingly awkward moments with Duncan, who sensed the growing happiness in me as clearly as I sensed the deepening misery in him. But the practicalities of the situation were that the property market was flat and, having been jilted virtually at the altar by his previous girlfriend/fiancée, Andrew wasn't quite there yet with the full-on commitment. So we carried on as we were, playing the push-me pull-me of the dating game full-on.

I arranged to take Andrew on a horse-riding weekend. Instead of turning up on his motorbike he arrived in a Morris Minor convertible, borrowed from an eccentric Primetime friend, and we dawdled down to the Cotswolds with the promise of sun on our faces and the wind in our hair, laughing all the way. I could see he was nervous but trying manfully to hide it.

I couldn't resist it. 'Horses can tell if you're anxious by the way.'

He drummed his fingers on the steering wheel.

'Perhaps a couple of pints tomorrow, before we mount?' I suggested, stifling my giggles.

'Perhaps tonight, too,' he grinned, turning the Vivaldi up on the stereo. 'Before and after we mount.'

The late sun dappled us as we passed under leaning trees, heavy with leaves. I navigated us through to our tiny village. We unpacked a few items and tested the springs on the wooden four poster bed. As the sun disappeared below the purple-heathered hills behind us we headed for the local, reached by climbing a steep path behind the farmhouse. Two hours later Andrew raced ahead of me and began to "ski" down the scree layered over the path.

'Do you ski, Di?' he called as he disappeared into the night air.

'Will you come ski-iiiing... with.... Meeeee?' he yelled, his voice getting fainter and fainter.

'Of course I will,' I shouted into the dark, shivering slightly at the all-enveloping darkness.

Despite his nerves, Andrew did well in the required riding lesson the next morning and was allowed out with me on an afternoon hack up into the Gloucestershire hills. I had a prancy chestnut mare, aptly named Twitch, and enjoyed showing off my riding skills. We reached the grassy crest of a hill. Tensing up for the next canter, I turned and smiled broadly at Andrew from under my jockey hat. He grinned back with a sheepish determination, his legs dangling comically down almost to the ground on his sturdy bay mare.

The panoramic countryside was all around us and the air, dense with heat on the roads, was refreshing that high up. I breathed in, deeply contented. Even though he didn't quite look like my knight in shining armour, there was no getting away from those sexy thighs against horse flesh, taut beneath his stretchy ski trousers.

I tapped Twitch into a canter. Andrew rose to the challenge and, with the rest of the pack of riders, caught up a few minutes later. I stood in the saddle to stretch my legs and clucked gently to my horse, revelling in the uncomplicated happiness that so often eludes us.

CHAPTER SIX

Alive and (no) Kicking

I awoke to a soft light and the sound of gentle electronic beeping. Waves of peace, free from pain, swept over me. Life flooded into my senses. I tingled and vibrated with life-force and sheer, pure energy: soothed, calm and very much alive.

My sister Helen stood at the side of my bed watching me. Her face was strained, grey with grief and tears.

'Helg! I'll be alright! I promise!'

The morphine made my tongue work. It brought humour.

'They've chopped my foot off. I'm going to look like Long John Silver, aren't I?'

The response was a loud, sudden sob. A choking, wretched, noise from my sister.

I frowned. How could I have caused such grief? I tried to raise my head but my throat scorched with pain. I winced. I couldn't swallow. What is this?

I looked down at my legs. Pure white sheets covered the bed, raised by a cage that lifted the covers neatly off the mattress. Everything was hidden by the swathe of material. I didn't know what was there. Or what wasn't.

I looked back up, but Helen had vanished. Replaced by a woman with a patient face, standing over me.

'Diana,' she said softly. 'Do you know what happened to you?'

The image of my leg lying away from me on the track surfaced. Terror replaced the morphed-up cosiness of the moments before.

But I had to face up to this. 'Yes. I was in a train accident. I've lost my leg haven't I?' I rallied, nodding towards the construction that covered the lower half of my body.

She took my hand. Her touch was cool and dry.

'Diana, that's right.'

I took in her words. So it was true. I had lost my leg. But what was this? She was staring into my eyes, 'Diana?'

I blanched, looked up and met her concerned gaze full-on. No? I said without words, no – not more bad news? Surely?

I liked her voice and her eyes were kind, but then I noticed the black robes and the white band around her neck. Sod it, no – a dog collar. This woman was a vicar, a hospital vicar. Here to pray for good news – mainly because she made it her business to be in places where good news was in short supply. She was here to bring me more bad news.

'Can you tell me what happened to your other leg?'

Deep in my soul, where not even the strongest dose of morphine could ever take hold, cold fear took over. The silent scream that exploded into my stomach, my chest, was akin to an internal *Munch* portrait. That inner scream would not melt away for many months and somehow I knew this. I thought of my dad, trundling him along the hospital corridors in that cumbersome, ugly wheelchair. My chest tightened. 'No legs.' My brain screamed at me. 'I have NO legs at ALL.'

'I don't have a leg to stand on? Is that what you're telling me,' I found myself saying, cool as anything and shocking myself. The way humour, gallows and otherwise, would bubble up at the most inappropriate moments was to become a remarkable, bizarre, feature of my new life but I didn't know that yet.

She smiled, puffing out a laugh, or was it a cry, in a choking exhale. Her name was Hilary. She was a lovely woman, all maternal bosom under a starchy black and white religious uniform.

'Diana will rise like a phoenix, I can sense it,' she said to my mum later, and I loved her for it.

Two policemen had gone to my parents' home. Mum stayed up all night until the trains were running to bring her to me. Cleaning the whole house over and over, the nesting instinct re-established of a mother before birth. She was a mother praying for a re-birth.

She'd tried to phone the surgeons, eventually getting put through to the ante-room next to the operating theatre.

'Please save her other leg,' she had pleaded.

'I'm sorry Mrs Hill, we're trying to save your daughter's life.'

My right leg had been ripped off below the knee. My left leg crushed and electrocuted, was amputated above the knee that night. I was in theatre for over eight hours. My body had been fed 12 pints of blood.

When I came round I retained an incredible sense of being alive, as if I'd been dead and had returned, although I didn't know where I'd been. There was some talk later from the surgeons that, although it had obliterated my left leg, the electricity had possibly saved my life, cauterising the horrific damage done by the being trapped under the train wheel for over 40 minutes. The combination of soaring amounts of adrenaline and electric shocks had somehow merged to keep me out of the type of shock that kills.

I was in intensive care for 36 hours. I remember two other patients. One man, suffering from third degree burns, expelled the death rattle from his mouth. The other, a younger man, had been in a light aircraft crash. I was glad to be out of there. But this tiny amount of pleasure was soon ripped away. As I was being pushed on a trolley through the hospital corridors to take up residence in my own room, I heard one nurse ask another what had happened to me.

'Poor love, she did what any of us could do,' came the reply. 'Got on a moving train...'

I lifted my head in indignation. Hey no, that's not what happened! I opened my mouth to say but they'd gone.

Visitors flocked in, an endless stream of talk, of gossip, jokes, presents, cards and flowers. Family and friends manicured the filthy dirt of the railway track from my nails, washed my hair, brought gifts of perfumes, choccies, books, magazines and letters. I even had a Visitor's Book, organised by Helen. Never had I had so much attention and felt so loved and wanted. They came alone, in small groups and large parties offering comfort and solace, waking me from my narcotic-ridden dreams and willing me to get better. They needed to see me, to see that I was going to be alright and I have no doubts at all that they initiated my first stage of recovery.

Every day they tidied my room and helped me to brush my hair and teeth. We talked of life outside, a world I had been so abruptly pulled away from. Sometimes I could see outside the window and didn't understand what was happening out there. My own world had become so small, a microcosm of what had been before.

Some people, desperately trying to understand how I felt, would come and talk of some injury or pain they'd endured in their life to try and put it on scale to my agony. They wanted and needed to empathise on a very deep level. Neil, a close boyfriend from my university days, said something I shall never forget: 'If I or any of us could take some of this pain away from you and give it to ourselves we would,' and added with tears in his eyes, 'I wish I could take all of the pain.'

It was unusual for any visitor to see me in chronic suffering. The drugs were, on the whole, administered effectively. Most of the time there was a joyful shindig happening where we would all laugh our way through an evening at the hilarious incidents that happened almost on a daily basis. Most of the events I would describe revolved around the brilliance or gross incompetence of the nursing and medical staff. For in hospital, I came to realise, there are no angels or devils, there are professionals and incompetents, with a few mavericks in between. As in life, the best and the worst worked and lived together.

Flowers began to arrive too. Massive armfuls of fragrant colour. I smelt every bunch, fondled every bouquet as I read the cards attached. The first display to arrive was from Paddy, a friend of Helen's, who is a lawyer. The suspicions as to the cause of the accident had already begun to permeate the hospital conversations. Paddy told Helen to act quickly.

She went down to the station with some home-made signs. She was stopped and questioned but thankfully it was an empathetic platform manager, a woman as it happened, rather than a jobsworth. Upon hearing Helen's mission, she turned a blind eye and Helen was able to stick the signs up on the platform without hindrance.

Accident 9th August: A woman fell beneath the Victoria train on platform 2 at approximately 6.30pm. Did you see anything? Call Helen Hill on ……

CHAPTER SEVEN

Torn Between Two Lovers

When I saw Andrew standing at the end of my bed my first reaction was surprise.

What the f***'s he doing here? (Swearing took on a life of its own in my new, restricted circumstances – a powerful, necessary, release valve.)

I'm no longer beautiful. I no longer deserve a man or have a future.

Do I?

My initial surprise was followed by euphoric relief.

Maybe I do? He was here. He'd *come*!

I had to make him stay now. I'd do everything in my power to make him stay. This man who'd known me as I was before, tall and beautiful, was my only chance of any future as a woman, as a lover, a mother. I'd attracted him and got him. Keeping him would now be my number one task.

Ever since my father's accident and then Becky's pregnancy the urge for a baby had grown. More than anything else in my life I wanted to settle down. Pre-accident, post-accident, nothing had changed on that score and that one hope, at least, hadn't been taken away from me. Yet. Everything, absolutely all of my future happiness now rested on Andrew.

'I will be alright, I will be,' I promised him. Over and over I repeated the words to Andrew, as he stood white with shock, his head bowed, his voice strained in that reverence to the seriously ill I was becoming so familiar with.

Then Duncan turned up.

Dunky! Even Duncan wouldn't want me now, I thought. I was wrong, he was still deeply in love with me, but that didn't matter. This would now make it easier for him to eventually move on. And Andrew was here. He'd come to me. Look they were talking, meeting, man to man instead of dodging each other in our tiny attic flat.

How strange that it took such tragedy for everything to come right. My problems of before were no longer. Duncan was my friend. Andrew was my lover. They were here together as people who were in my life. Who cared for me.

'I must have some water, please.' The nurses assented to allow me ice cubes which I sucked at greedily, an oasis of water for my wretched throat. Duncan and Andrew had to call for a bowl as the icy water was regurgitated, bringing with it a flow and then clots of blood. I became aware of the number of drips attached to me. Fourteen lines hooked and fed into my hands and arms, veins and arteries routed to the roads of lines that led to bottles and plastic bags hung above me. Eight glass containers were planted around the base of my bed, draining off fluids.

There's little time for genuine rest in hospital. It's a busy cycle of nurses carrying out treatments, bed-baths, blood pressures, dressing checks, changing of pumps and drips. I was "disturbed" a minimum of every one to two hours, twenty-four hours a day.

In those early days in hospital I didn't deal with it personally at all. Whilst the body took over and attempted to begin the healing process, the brain function remained a little behind. And while it tried to sort things out, to put the new perspectives and parameters into place, it reacted strongly.

Over a particular few days not even the Diamorphine that was being fed directly into me through one of the drips was enough to quell the tortuous racking of pain that crashed its way through my body. A doctor prescribed an anti-epileptic drug with the understanding that it was the crucified nerves that were generating such appalling sensations. The combination of these drugs put me, quite simply, on another planet. Daliesque landscapes appeared, tiny leering dwarf faces, distorted and misshapen. I began to fear closing my eyes. Every time I blinked a new horror would turn up.

The vivid colours were always in red and black: twisted limbs, curtains of blood, waterfalls of blood, the colours of hell. They were visions, hysterical, dreadful and totally fearful. I didn't understand where they came from, I'd never seen sights like them before. The brain was clearly trying to do its work, to sort it out, like a computer chucking up material from the unknown, the sinister subconscious. They gave me more sleeping tablets. Still I would not sleep. I kept my eyes looking straight ahead, not daring to close them.

I loved the majority of the nurses tending to me. It took six of them to lift me, they were so careful and tender. I got to know the names of their boyfriends and husbands. There were lots of earthy discussions about sex and bodily functions. I felt I had to assist them in their tasks that frequently caused me pain.

My chest hurt and I whimpered one day as they tried to move me for washing. They soothed and comforted and plumped my pillows. What they didn't tell me was that I'd broken half my ribs. I discovered this a long time later, a piece of news from a solicitor. They hadn't told me because they could do nothing about it and it was the least of my worries.

I was receiving visitors all day and into the evening but then the horrors of being alone with my new and terrible injuries would plague me all night.

One night two girlfriends were with me, holding my hand, murmuring, being strong for themselves and therefore for me. I felt the drugs physically take hold. I was aware of a gradual slipping away in to the land of chronic hallucination. The alarming experience of these delusions is that they are real, that was my reality. The walls began to move, shifting inwards and any speech I had left became slurred.

The girlfriends had to leave. I was left alone with "Imelda", a night-shifter with a face like Imelda Marcos and a clipped, cool manner that almost bordered on pathological hatred. She despised me for having so many visitors during the day and early evening. There was often almost a party atmosphere in my room, as I discussed amusing anecdotes from hospital life with friends. Her shift, which started at about 9pm, was disturbed. She didn't like the banter and laughter. She wanted peace and quiet, to be able to sit, and probably sleep, at her desk.

Because I was in my own room, visitors were allowed in the evenings. This meant she had to attend to me for blood pressure readings and temperature gauging surrounded by a small audience. It was Imelda who kept me waiting on the night that the morphine drip ran out. The drugs closed in on me. Horrendous pain, combined with the hallucinatory powers of the anti-epileptic drug made my brain play in slow motion the scenes from the accident I had mercifully not experienced in total at the time. The colossal crushing weight of the train. The heavy juddering of the electricity and, worse, the moment that the train ripped off my right leg.

Minute after minute ticked by as I rang the bell in a fearful panic. I actually felt the unstemmed flow of blood running down my leg, which was on back to front. I became hysterical with fear. The previously pleasant aroma of hundreds of flowers became overpowering and sickly. The smell became the stench of death, filling my head. They were arranged around my room and as the living nightmare increased, they began to make the bed smaller. They became my funeral flowers and my bed shrunk to a wooden box, a coffin. I knew then why people had been so wonderful to me, showering love and good wishes. It was because I was dying.

I kept my finger on the bell, attached to a piece of rope I would dearly have liked to hang myself with if it had been long enough. Still the nurse did not come. Was she waiting for me to die? Or was I dead already? I began to call, feebly at first, but then a full scream of panic and crying out for my sister Helen.

Imelda soft-footed her way into my room and stood at the door, her colleague a sinister shadow behind her.

'Stop making such a noise Miss Hill, you're disturbing the other patients.'

'I'm in agony and I want to see my sister. I'm dying. Please help me.'

'It's 3 in the morning. I don't think you should disturb your sister. We're here to look after you. What do you need? You seemed to be fine earlier.'

'She said I could phone at any time. I want to see my sister,' I cried, tears of confusion and desperation pouring down my cheeks.

'I'll have to get a ward sister to change the pump.'

'I don't want you I want my sister GET ME MY SISTER,' I called out, shocking them with the ferocity of delivery.

'Not possible,' said she with all the power, arms crossed in defiance.

'Bitch!' I yelled. 'Incompetent cow. GET ME MY SISTER!'

They left and a few minutes later a night sister, called from another ward, came to my room. She was soothing with kind hands and warm words. I began to feel better but the terrors were still there, threatening to change the room back into a funeral parlour. She asked me questions in a sing-song Irish voice and I forced myself to answer, trying to focus on reality.

'Do you smoke?' she asked as she efficiently changed the drug pump.

'I did, but I'm trying to give up,' I sobbed.

She turned off the oxygen points in the room, opened a window and lit me a cigarette.

I inhaled tentatively. An old habit and a remnant from a sane life. My mind began to clear. Reality began to creep its way into the room.

This incident became a pattern in my life. The caring competent nurses of the day-time shifts were often taken over at night by the dragons, incompetents and frequently stupid part-timers with no experience.

43

One night, on the eve of an important operation, one of a whole series I was to have in this hospital, a small makeshift bed was assembled with permission given for a visitor to stay overnight.

I lay back on my bed, watching Duncan and Andrew arguing as to who was going to have the pleasure of sleeping in my room, both unaware that they would be endlessly disturbed on the hour for the blood pressure and temperature gauging.

The head-devil was still with me from my night-traumas and I couldn't help but be amused at this spat taking place in front of me. Perhaps my constitution reacted well with the morphine-based drugs. Some it would make sick, some sedated to the point of permanent sleep. With me it made me talk my little head off, about anything.

I'd never been one to talk like a twittering parrot. I kept going on about wanting a bird for my shoulder, an outer display of handling the fact that I had lost one leg, but not both. I continually laid claim to being like Long John Silver and imagined myself hobbling around on a wooden leg, dressed in an outfit to match with an eye-patch for extra effect. Adding to my amusement, and deepest affection for Andrew that evening – a powerful aphrodisiac in our relationship was a shared, similar sense of humour – was a large blown-up parrot he'd brought in with him. When he wasn't there I would attach it to my arm with a string and talk to it.

'I'll stay the night,' said Andrew, a hint of resignation seeping through his words.

'No, I will,' said Duncan. 'Might as well, it's a long way back to Bromley. I can go straight to work from here.'

'Who do you want to stay?' Helen, my mediator, asked me.

Though I was thinking it would be nice to have Andrew sleep over, I shrugged my shoulders and raised my eyes to the ceiling.

'I'll stay,' Duncan repeated. 'I don't mind sleeping here.'

Andrew looked relieved.

'OK Dunky it is,' I concurred. Though disappointed, I was also relieved as I felt that to reveal any semblance of neediness was dangerous. I believed that if I could somehow prove some type of independence, Andrew would still want me.

The next morning I was rolled off into the anteroom for the slight scratch of anesthesia that pulled me away from the world and into the slow countdown into the void of the theatre room. I had no fear of the impending operation. They were making things better. I'd be knocked out for the count. Wouldn't I?

44

When I half-awoke I was not in theatre, but in a racing pit, surrounded by white and green coated racing drivers stripping layer after layer of flesh from my legs, setting fire and watching them burn. I was trying to scream at them but couldn't. They couldn't hear me, or chose not to. They were telling jokes, about Niki Lauda, laughing at my abject pain and misery. I was in hell, a burning flesh-rotting inferno that became a large room, with people all around me on trolleys, whimpering with pain. Two people, their nose and mouth masks hanging down on their green uniforms, stood casually beside me discussing canteen food. I could speak by then but they couldn't comprehend the distress I was in. It felt like a massive room, peopled by hundreds of dying soldiers, like a scene from MASH. Green uniforms, countless beds, crying people in hellish agony.

I was crying with distress when Duncan suddenly appeared at the bottom of my bed. I was back in my room.

'Dunky, I've been to hell. I've seen it.'

'Come on now Di, you've had an operation. I'm here. Don't worry.'

The visions wouldn't leave me. I asked to see the consultant who'd been in attendance at the operation.

He stood by the side of the bed, his face full of question.

'I was awake,' I said fixing my eyes on him.

'You were well under Diana.'

'You were telling jokes.'

He blanched slightly.

'Jokes about racing drivers,' I went on. 'My legs were on fire. There was a joke about Niki Lauda.'

He went quite pale and became very still.

'We will be extremely careful with anaesthetics next time. I am sorry. I'll let Roehampton know.'

My temperature roared up. I tried to explain that it was probably the operation process that had caused this, but they considered there was an infection. Down I went again for my next operation, shuddering with terror into the tunnel of hell. The pre-med I had asked for seemed to have no effect. This time I did stay under, they re-checked and re-did the dressings again. I came to out of the anaesthesia feeling OK. They upped the antibiotics dosage, fed into a drip tap, one of four plugged into my hands.

Then came the news that was to rock me for the next 5 years.

CHAPTER EIGHT

You're Holding My Heart – Diana Hill

Seven days after the accident my sister Helen tentatively placed a newspaper on the bed, the top, bold, headline on the front page.
'I thought you'd better see this.'

RAIL FALL WOMAN FACES COURT THREAT
A 29-year-old London woman faces prosecution after falling down the edge of the platform and losing both of her legs. She was running to catch a train when the accident took place last week at Wandsworth Town Station. A spokesman for British Transport Police said 'She tried to get on a moving train and we will be interviewing her with a view to prosecution. We can't say exactly when this will be at the moment.' British Rail recently put out a public warning to passengers to discourage them from boarding trains that were already leaving the station: 'The risk just isn't worth it. The chances of serious injury or death are too high – just a small loss of balance or a slip and they can fall down between the train and the platform and incur horrific injuries. The worst offenders are commuters...'

Disbelief was followed by anger.
'That's a lie!' I cried, sobbing in fury. 'It was still. The train was still!'
'We know, we know that Di.'
'Worst *offenders*. Faces *prosecution*?' I couldn't believe what I was reading. 'How can they do that?'
'Try not to worry. We're acting on it, I've got Paddy on the case.'
With the help of her lawyer friend, Helen had already started a frantic search for good legal representation.
They didn't mention me by name, other newspaper headlines referred to me throughout as the Fall-Girl. Flickers of emotional fire surged through

me – The Fall Girl! How unbelievably insensitive was that? How could they dare release such a public statement with no reference to my side of events?

I felt crucified and stupid. The accident ran over and over again in my mind, releasing further pain. With the pain came clarity. I felt myself fall slowly down the side of the train. The nano seconds it takes for a body to be changed was to become a recurring nightmare. Just before I fell asleep at night I relived the seconds before that moment, the gush of the train. I saw no guard. I heard no warning. The train was stationary when I got on.

I became convinced more than ever that something had gone wrong with the British Rail safety procedure. The aggressive stance "leaked" to that newspaper from the British Rail source, rather than by direct contact with myself or my relatives, also made me horribly aware that they were going on the attack. This was clearly either a pre-emptive strike to stop any litigation procedure or a warning that it would be too difficult to contemplate suing them. Their decision not to name me in their report was another indicator. If they had, of course, I could have sued.

I wanted Helen to arrange for the newspaper reporters to interview me, so I could deliver my side of this one-sided nonsense. I reached for my make-up bag.

'I will get all lippyed-up and tell them what's what.'

But I fell back into the comfort of the pillows, exhausted at the prospect. And some inner voice saying this was not the right thing to do. What if it did go to court?

A judge may not look favourably on someone that was shooting their (lippeyed) mouth off.

I was now the JFK of Bromley, Kent. Everyone who knew the real identity of the Fall-Girl remembered exactly where they were and what they were doing when they were told of my accident. It was another major difficulty to deal with, like being inside my own living obituary.

From a young age I'd always had an inner feeling that I would be famous. A great many people suffer from this ailment, even more so today with our celebrity culture gone rampant. I've never got to grips with the reasoning behind my own ambition to jump on this dubious bandwagon. Maybe because I'm the middle child and was striving for attention.

I sang for a while with a band of hopeful anarchist hippies called Trieb, which means desire in German. They imagined themselves as trailblazing revolutionaries, but in reality we sang good old favourites like *Brown Sugar* and *Wishing Well*. I say I sang, it was more of a boo wop wop with another dark haired "girlie" called Kate. I embroidered red poppies onto our white linen blouses – our stage outfits – and wore the tightest white jeans I could.

I also featured in a couple of fashion shows. This all came about via a local upmarket hairdresser in Wilmslow, my hometown. The guy who did my hair was taking rather a long time. There was a lot of hair stroking and pulling of locks around my face in different styles. He kept standing behind me, his crotch pressed to my back, admiring us both in the mirror. I was expecting him to lunge at me any minute. It got to half past seven in the evening and he kept putting *Romeo and Juliet* by Dire Straits on the salon's trendy stereo with massive speakers. Eventually he did lunge – verbally – with a 'would you like to model some clothes in our local fashion show?' I was so relieved I said yes. Two weeks later I was strutting my stuff down a cobbled-together catwalk in the local town hall.

Some of the clothes were wonderful and I enjoyed myself thoroughly until a fight broke out backstage. Someone had nicked someone's hat.

'Give us me hat, yer bitch,' screeched one model.

'It's mine, yer tart,' screamed another, as posh northern accents were temporarily dropped for broad Manchester.

I don't know why but I joined in. I felt the stirrings of Prima Donna'ism rising within me and it could not be quelled. I grabbed the offending hat and put it on my head yelling 'it suits me better than either of you two slags,' and tottered off onto the stage.

I was modelling a cream skirted suit. The hat didn't match and as I strutted the cream jacket fell off my shoulders. I gracefully bent over to pick up the jacket and the hat fell off. The audience laughed and all ideas about being a catwalk model ended there. Much to my relief. I was genuinely frightened at my personality change. Not that I was shy and retiring but I didn't want to be a bitch.

And then there was my determined effort to become a singer. In my late teens through to my early 20's I had been writing songs, and, aged 23, had engineered a recording of one of them – *You're Holding My Heart*, and then managed to blag a slot with an A&R talent spotting guy at a well-known record company. He listened to my four track warblings, switched it off and turned to look at a massive poster adorning his office wall.

'Not quite Madonna, is it Diana?'

My fantasies about being famous didn't leave me until my late twenties when I began to live the most wonderful working life. From 1987, transported to Cannes, Monte-Carlo, Los Angeles, New York, interviewing the rich, the very rich and the famous, as journalists we could rub shoulders and interact with their glamour. You're so busy living your life you don't have time to think about what you would fantasise about doing. Now here I was, The Fall-Girl, lying in a hospital bed. Famous for all the wrong reasons.

The effect of my tragedy on others was horrifying. I had to relive the emotions of the loss of my limbs with every single new visitor who arrived. The shock waves travel like an atomic bomb. I heard these tales of horror and distress gradually over the months, some even years later. Some haven't been able to tell me to this day.

I was lucky in one profound aspect. Many of my friends are either journalists, authors or actors, people used to taking on board circumstance beyond the normal life experience. They weren't frightened of asking questions. These weren't queries of a prurient nature but designed to get at the truth.

When Barbie and Christine came into intensive care for example, I was able to go through the journey with them, step by step. Christine confessed much later that her knees were knocking she was so fearful as to what state I would be in. I was dealing with the utmost horror, I didn't have to wonder how I came to be injured. I knew what had happened. I saw everything. And the more I told my tale of tragedy, the less potent it eventually became.

It was my beloved mum who helped to carry this sometimes overwhelming state of guilt. She, now a full-time carer to my father, still rang every day, wrote letters and somehow gave me the strength to endure.

If she can bear it, these insurmountable feelings of loss and grief, then so can I. She travelled down to me whenever she could. I considered the courage this took – two of her closest family crippled by accidents. One by a train.

I felt wholly responsible for my visitors' grief and did my utmost to help them carry the burden of it, to come to terms with it themselves. I had to be strong for everyone else. Later I was to discover this is a common natural anaesthetic, transferring the trajectory of my personal horror onto others' emotions. These feelings of second-hand loss in them were real enough, of course. But unbeknownst to me I was delaying the time when I'd have to deal with my own deepest, most profound, grief until years later.

There would have been no way round this even if I'd known – my capabilities of coming to terms with my new reality were on full-stretch as it was.

Then came the call I didn't, with all my heart, want to come. Andrew was my focus now, but nevertheless the familiar whomp in my stomach returned with full force when, just after dinner one day, Sister Jackie from Limb Surgery Reception rushed into my room.

'There's a man on the phone from New York,' she said breathlessly. A flush of inner pride absorbed my shock for a moment. The deep, sexy tone of Max's voice had clearly been working its magic on her, too.

CHAPTER NINE

In The Stone

Sarah was in the room with me at the time. I was in no fit state to go to the phone or to speak to him. Mobile phones weren't widely available then and even the hospital facilities didn't stretch to plug-in bedside receivers.

Thank God.

What was there to say? Our relationship had always been so physical. He made me feel so beautiful, inside and out. Now I didn't have the words. I didn't know what words of comfort I could have said to him to make it better for him.

He'd heard via the editor of a UK TV magazine. She had a friend who worked at his company who told him his "girlfriend" had just been killed.

'What?'

'Oh, she's not quite dead yet, but it looks like she's gonna die.'

Well, at least he knew now that I wasn't going to die. That would have to be enough.

Nurse Jackie returned with his message.

'Will you tell Diana that I love her?'

I felt joy. I knew it was too late so it was a joy tinged with sadness. But he hadn't said it before, those kinds of words had never been a part of our particular erotic dance. The rehab that would soon start with Roehampton's world-renown team of rehabilitation specialists – learning to walk again, learning to cope with the world as an invalid – all centred around my future life with Andrew.

I had no idea how complex a task putting one false foot in front of the other was going to be at that time. Laughably, I thought it would be strap me up and go. I'd already decided that my main mission after walking would be to get back to riding on Andrew's motorbike. And that never faltered. I was determined to get back the life that we'd lost and nothing less.

News of the anonymous Fall-Girl's accident spread at a furious pace as the original article was picked up by all the other Nationals. I went over and over the events as the newspapers had reported them and how I remembered them. I knew for certain that the train had been stationary. There was no way that particular memory could twist into a "perhaps" or a "maybe I was mistaken". No matter how boldly it was written otherwise for all the world to see.

I've never been a rash person, and that is what these articles were implying. It was an initial hint of the viciousness to come. My journalist friends and I discussed what form this might take. Several of them phoned British Rail and the newspapers. Michael Winner, who I'd come to know through his personal assistant, my close friend Dinah, wrote a letter to one of them:

What unbelievable insensitivity for a Transport Police spokesman to announce to your paper (16 August) that a young lady who has just lost both her legs under a train at Wandsworth Station will be interviewed with a view to being prosecuted.

One would have thought that even if she was running to catch the train, having both legs ripped off while she lay on the track was punishment enough. I happen to know the young woman involved and the cause of the accident is, I believe, to be disputed. She is, of course, in deep and terrible shock at being crippled for life.

The police, Transport and otherwise, are going through a rough time. They require, and I think in general deserve, the support of the public. This sort of cruel and tacky behaviour will not help. Michael Winner, Sackville Street, W1

This is very Michael Winner. Forthright and to the point. There was little messing with someone like Michael and his letter, published on the Letters Page, demanded a response, which was forthcoming, the withdrawal of prosecution addressed to the media's readers, not me. I never heard from them directly.

John Prescott, the then Transport Secretary brought it up in Parliament, also questioning the cruelty.

Because of all this pressure, and I'm positive only because of the high clout-level of my defenders of truth, British Rail eventually retracted their statement.

Michael Winner told Dinah that it was absolutely imperative to get a good lawyer for the ensuing fight. He offered his own, who were of course prohibitively expensive. Helen's friend Paddy had come through with a lead on a good personal injury firm and Helen's boyfriend, Jonny, and Andrew bravely ventured to the scene of the accident to take photos as a precursor to establishing evidence.

'Not much there,' said Jonny. 'A couple of batteries and your pen.' He handed me the pen. I looked in horrified wonder at it, unable to comprehend that the last time I used it I had been someone with both legs.

They'd taken some more fliers with them which was just as well because all of Helen's had been taken down.

They'd managed to get onto the platform without being apprehended and got some photos of the track – the spot where I fell right down was still covered in blood-stained sawdust. They told me how surprised they were at how far it was from the bottom of the steps where I'd tried to board the train. That the guard hadn't seen me for all that distance as I was wedged between the platform and the moving train was unfathomable.

A train arrived and, amazingly, as they were handing out the fliers, a man who'd seen the accident approached them.

'I saw it,' he said. 'A girl tried to get on the train but it started and she fell.'

I wanted to rise from my wheelchair and jump up and down when they told me this. Instead, I yelped, with delight. It was the most tremendous relief to hear somebody else verify actually what had happened.

'Did you get his phone number?'

'Er, no…'

'WHAT?'

'He raced off, it all happened so fast. We can find him again…' said Andrew. 'He's got our number, we gave him the flier,' added Jonny. 'He's a black guy, and obviously a regular commuter…'

'Did you find anybody else?'

'The man in the ticket booth.'

'The BR man?'

'Mr Levi, we got his name. He was friendly and empathetic…'

'Hmm… what did he say?'

'He said you ran past but the train had already set off when you went by him.'

'*What?*'

'That's what we said,' said Jonny, anxiously reaching for my hand.

Andrew looked awkward and embarrassed. 'He said you stood no chance of catching it.'

'The fucking *lying* bastard.'

'I think he was...' Andrew began.

'He couldn't even *see* the train from that booth, did you not tell him that?'

'Er...'

'Bring on the lawyers that's all I can say.'

I was grateful to them both and the man's statement gave me some hope, but this was a major disappointment. One true witness who saw what really happened so near but so far; another mistaken witness in the employ of British Rail and their bunch of incompetents.

In case you think my anger towards the whole of British Rail and its employees was skewed by my personal tragedy, it might be worth mentioning here another avoidable accident caused by human error. The Clapham Junction rail disaster happened less than two years before mine at a time when morale at BR was already at an all-time low. This is from the Wikipedia entry on the investigation into the horrifying collisions of three trains on 12 December 1988 which killed 35 and injured 500:

"The immediate cause of the crash was incorrect wiring work in which an old wire, incorrectly left in place after rewiring work and still connected at the supply end, created a false feed to a signal relay. The larger cause of the accident was the failure by British Rail senior management to recognise that the re-signalling of the Clapham Junction area – and indeed the re-signalling of all the lines out of Waterloo, of which this was a part – should have been treated as a major, safety-critical project, controlled throughout by a single, senior, named project manager. Instead the job was left to middle-level technical staff, stressed, poorly supervised by their seniors and poorly supported by their juniors. Staffing levels were inadequate and the staff, dulled by months of voluntary seven-days-a-week work, were carrying out the complete re-signalling of the largest and, on some measures, busiest junction on the whole British rail system..."

Incorrect wiring work = human error.

I understand that the majority of the causes of these crashes and accidents comes down, on close investigation, to human error. As this deeply flawed nationalised industry limped towards privatisation and my accident, morale – and safety standards – weren't likely to be on any upward trajectory, put it that way. In the post-Clapham months leading up to my accident, the Purley rail crash killed 6 and injured 94; the collision of 2 commuter trains at Glasgow Bellgrove killed 2; the Newton rail accident, also in Glasgow, killed 4 and injured 22. British Rail was tired and run-down. Appearances on the run-up to privatisation were everything. No matter that mine had been ruined.

In polar opposition to the underhand sideswipes from British Rail, my family and friends were making me feel very valuable as a person, which is all someone needs in such circumstance. I was made to feel heroic, courageous and strong. I was going to bounce back and most people, knowing me, believed in me.

Somehow, with sheer courage and nerves of steel, my father made it down, by train, to visit me. He was still very unwell himself, but phone calls and my dear Ma's relaying of how well I was doing were not enough. He needed to see me, and sat, defeated by the long hospital corridor walk, in a wheelchair. I wheeled in, and my humour at the blasted irony that we should both meet again, in wheelchairs, was lost on me. I clung to him, sobbing, whispering 'My daddy, my daddy'. A man of few words, he uttered barely anything. I felt like Roberta in, and this is highly ironic, *The Railway Children*, when she sees her father for the first time after his release from prison. Dad and I were both now in a prison of sorts. Would we ever be free?

Other visitors, some not so loved by me, made their way to my hospital room.

There were a few odd remarks that came at me out of the blue. Someone stated, very thoughtfully, that if they were me, they wouldn't want to live.

This got me questioning through the dark hours of pain-wracked, sleepless nights. Did I want to live?

Survival, to live and to breathe and knowing that I hadn't died were the only facts I could concentrate on with any certainty. The majority of my friends would never dwell on the practical and emotional challenges ahead but these loaded, unintentionally hurtful questions remained with me, especially when I was alone. Trying to answer them put me into a crushing state of panic. Where was I going to live? Would I ever work again? Would

I walk again? And what of Andrew? He came in often. He smiled and joked but rarely did we have time for a "proper" chat. The future seemed a taboo subject.

The drugs made me very affectionate. I loved everyone. Emotion filled my heart and soul and I reached out mentally and physically to anybody I knew would return it. People told me what they thought of me and I was stunned at their kind words. My brother said he loved me – for the first time ever. There were frequent scenes straight from some American movie where everyone tells each other they love each other. We meant it, though, from the depths of our despair.

My perspective on the world was set at those two extremes. The tremendous love and demonstrable affection for me, in person and via the kind of letters and cards written with the same sort of emotion that surges up at the time of bereavement; rubbing right up against the growing sense of indignation and shock at the stings which crept through to me from the world outside the hospital windows. Though I had truth on my side, the additional grief precipitated by the British Rail statement filled me with paranoia. Wondering if I was going slightly insane, I called for a psychiatrist.

She was a pleasant enough woman. She sat by my bed and listened to the tale of horror but then, all of a sudden, she started to ask questions about my childhood.

I became agitated. I couldn't fathom why she needed such personal detail on the past. Was she attempting to conclude that I may not have enough stability in my background to cope with such a life-changing event?

Rather than soothing my paranoia, she increased it. Survival, to live and to breathe and knowing that I hadn't died, were the only facts I could concentrate upon.

Revisiting my childhood, suddenly, out of the blue like that was a mistake. What had my childhood got to do with this horrific trauma? Nothing on earth I had ever experienced matched this.

'My childhood was perfect,' I wailed. 'I was so happy.' I broke down into such hysterical, deep, sobbing tears that she had to leave.

My childhood was idyllic.

I'd been born on the Wirral near Liverpool. We'd moved when I was nearly two so my first memories are all based around our home in Wilmslow in Cheshire.

We lived in a house that overlooked a golf course at the back and banked onto fields at the side in a quiet and peaceful cul-de-sac. There were local shops at the bottom of the road and schools were bus journeys away.

I was very close to my sister, Helen and rather distant from my brother, David, purely because of age differences. I'd knocked David off his perch with my arrival, four years after his, and Helen had knocked me off my little throne when I was two and a bit. I forgave her and we loved each other completely. Mum says I squealed with delight when I saw her, newly born in her cot, and scrambled across the bed to have a closer look. Big brown eyes and black hair. She looked like a monkey and I wanted to protect her. I called her Susy and would strap her into buckles and belts to keep her near to me. Happiness bubbles up in children like soft gasses from a volcano, unrelenting and startling. We fizzed with happiness. We roamed the fields surrounding the house and we were cherished by both parents.

Most of the time I played with Helen. If I happened to be alone I'd take my dolls Sindy and Paul walkabout in the fields, often dreaming up some scheme for them. A hollow in a tree was a whole house, a trickle of a stream a big dangerous river they had to cross. And they did a lot of kissing and cuddling. The imagination of a child knows no bounds, and I was highly imaginative.

Gangs of us would venture further than our given boundaries and dig dens by river banks. We'd half inch the spades from Dad's impeccably-kept tool shed and sneak off across the fields. Over "Butty Bank" and down into the forbidden territory beside the river. We dug and delved and ate apples and drank red "pop". In summer the fields became laden with hay bales and we'd stack them, square then of course, into the most amazing dens. We dreamed of our futures and schemed escapes further and further afield. Even then I had the sense of not wanting it to ever end. The freedom and security of a happy childhood.

In my drug-fuelled paranoia the happy memories began to twist – distorting into danger signals everywhere.

I'd christened the upstairs landing The Dangerous Road. Helen was never allowed to cross it on her own when I was about. I insisted she always wait for me to escort her in case she fell down the stairs.

'Don't fall. Don't FALL now!' I heard my mother's voice calling to me. 'Be CAREFUL FALL-GIRL...'

In the field my best friend Katy trod on a plank of wood with rusty nails. Dad had to remove the nails from her foot. 'Be CAREFUL now you girls,' I could hear my father's soft, concerned voice again.

I fell into a patch of nettles. I felt the stings again.

I got stuck trying to get out of David's tree house. I felt the intense shock of abandonment again. Why hadn't the train stopped for me? Why didn't they hear my screams?

I chopped through Katy's finger when we were digging by the river bank. Chop chop chop, finger off, blood blood blood… blood everywhere.

CHAPTER TEN

The Drugs Don't Work

I was still under the influence of the anaesthetic of yet another operation when a partner from Coopers, a firm of solicitors, came to visit.

Steve Hampshire was a youngish man with floppy brown hair, kind eyes and buckled teeth. He spoke softly, whispering questions weighted down with a reverence that people administer in the company of the ill.

He explained that his task on behalf of his firm was to establish the possibility of having a case against British Rail. I was quite heavily sedated, but managed to pull myself together enough for this crucial meeting. I immediately liked him and we got on well.

We discussed British Rail's action so far. Their lawyers and press people had fired the first cannon, going in on a public attack which had created the maximum distress, anxiety and fear in their victim. Designed, no doubt, to stop me suing them for malpractice. We discussed the suspicions my friends and I had about British Rail's upcoming privatisation. My accident had come at an unfortunate time for them. Their health and safety record was appalling. And I seemed to be yet another example of their alleged modus operandi – Blame the Passenger.

By the time of Steve's visit we knew that British Rail had decided not to hold an investigation. Of any kind. They weren't going to question the guard's story and they would not be seeking out witnesses. Their plan was to sweep it all away and move on. My reward being that I would not have the juggernaut of BR lawyers chasing me for a trespass fine. British Rail's reward would be good PR for not persecuting the victim. They'd have the added bonus of not having to garner a statement from me that would be holding up the truth in the face of their garbled version of events.

At first Steve was taken aback at my strong insistence that my accident was wholly BR's fault.

'I got on a stationary train which moved without warning,' I stated clearly. 'And when I fell the train didn't stop either. It kept going. Somebody wasn't doing their job properly.'

'I've read the witness statements,' Steve replied gently. 'And they all say "woman ran to catch a moving train ".'

My blood ran cold. 'what statements? What witnesses?'

'The driver. The guard...'

'Any passengers?'

'Er, no.'

Despite my hallucinatory mode and a tendency to go off at a tangent, especially when having to recall exactly how I ended up under the wheels of the train, there must have been some lucidity to my words. A few days later I heard that Coopers were going to take on my case.

We began to move swiftly. I had to brace myself for the task of unblocking the most painful memories imaginable to put into a full, written statement and we continued our search for witnesses.

My main priority so far had been the physical and emotional challenge of getting through the series of operations. There were to be five overall. Every time I was put under the anaesthetic I became filled with the fear and certainty that I was going to die. Alongside this, the challenge now began to clear my name. Memories I'd so dearly have loved to put behind me were going to have to be dredged up and placed under forensic examination.

Whilst I gathered the inner strength required to put my step by step account of my accident into writing, Steve, Andrew, my sister Helen and boyfriend Jonny set to work.

Every single passenger had had to get off the train and walk past me. Yet British Rail hadn't put any signs up. Some, like Maggie, the angel who'd come with me in the ambulance and had, I'm convinced, saved my life, were easy to find – she'd been back to visit. All I could say over and over was thank you, thank you, thank you. Others, like the man who'd come up to me as I lay under the train's wheel, would be much harder to track down.

The drugs kept the horrific pain at bay until, eleven days after I'd been admitted to St George's Hospital, Tooting, I was discharged. Quickly, and with little formality, I was unattached from my drips and carefully put into an ambulance.

I waved a tearful goodbye to the nurses I'd become very attached to. I insisted on taking a couple of teddies, armfuls of flowers, and, once again, tied the parrot to my arm. Mum was with me and Helen followed in her car.

As the journey began Mum and I kept up our usual banter, but then I started to feel very uncomfortable and fell silent. We came across a series of sleeping policemen in the road and I winced at every bump, conserving energy to endure the pain. I'd spent ten days on the most powerful cocktail of morphine and anti-epileptic – ie nerve calming – drugs, but I was transferred from the ambulance to the hospital on nothing. My cocooned state of false relaxation and comfort peppered with Salvador Dali landscapes had drained away. Without realising it I was effectively going cold turkey from the strongest of narcotics.

By the time we reached the ward I was climbing the walls in agony. This hurt was reality. My real world and what it had done to me. In a futile attempt to get a grip on the pain, every part of my body began to spasm.

So my introduction to Queen Mary's limb surgery ward was not a pleasant one. As I was trundled down a corridor I screamed and shrieked, banshee-like, for help, for somebody to PLEASE F-ING HELP ME. I wanted to run away from myself but that not being an option open to me anymore, metaphorically or otherwise, I'd have cheerfully accepted death instead.

A nurse gave me a shot of Diamorphine, I clawed at her uniform with my nails as she struggled to get the needle into my thigh. I felt more indignation. Why hadn't they warned me about the cold turkey? But then, maybe it was better that they hadn't.

Mum had to return to Cheshire, to Dad, but Helen stayed to help me settle into my new room. A nurse – a big cheerful lass from Newcastle called Alison – wired me up to the painkiller drips and I sank thankfully back into my own drugged up sanity. Sweetly, she immediately set about BluTacking all my cards onto the wall. I watched her, trying to make sense of my new surroundings.

This room was quiet compared to my last one, with only a distant hum of machinery, the whomp whomp of the ceiling fan and the distant sound of the nurses murmuring at the reception. It was painted a sickly pale green and the smell of disinfectant lingered in the air. I asked Helen to take me outside for some fresh air. As she pushed me along the corridor, the smell changed to cooking mixed with chemical floor cleaner, the aroma of the ill.

A sprawl of imposing, tall red-brick buildings with symmetric long, narrow windows and dirty old Nissan huts, Queen Mary's, Roehampton was founded in 1915 to provide care for wounded soldiers coming back from the Front. It has developed over the years into a world-renowned limb fitting and amputee rehabilitation centre, most famously featuring in *Reach for The Sky*, the classic movie about the World War II hero Douglas Bader starring Kenneth Moore. The mis-match of buildings, connected by pathways fringed by low box hedges and the odd lawn, looked more like a school than a hospital.

I was slightly disappointed. I'd pictured an old country house with a wooden porch, where my fellow inmates and I would pass time playing cards on patio tables while nurses with large hats would tend gracefully to our needs. This was of course a cine-picture imprinted on my mind from the film, where the gallantly injured heroes began a pleasant recovery period in comfort.

As my sister rolled me gently into the warmth of the late summer evening, a black mist of helplessness and despair came over me. For the first time I could sense Helen's sorrow at having to push her big sister in a wheelchair. I asked if she felt I would ever be happy again. She replied with tears streaming down her face that she did not know.

That's when the pain really began. And the realisation. During the day I kept up the banter but at night I cried and cried. Every night for months. Closing my eyes brought back images of hell, the stench of evil, blood everywhere.

CHAPTER ELEVEN

Praise

'Morning Diana. It's mid-morning oh sleepy one,' the lilting gay voice trickled through to my head. 'Welcome to Roehampton, a land of dressings and vicious nurses.'

I sat up to see a young man at the side of my bed dressed in white with a shock of dyed blonde hair. He had a large syringe in his hand and made dagger-like movements with it, the fluid dripping from the sharp needle onto the floor.

'Oh Jesus,' I muttered.

'No, Paul actually. Although some people think I'm heavenly,' and he raised his arms camply to flap the air, like the wings of an angel.

'Now then, just a little prick,' he grinned and came nearer with the syringe. I tensed and clenched my throat hard for the pain. He suddenly turned away and squirted the fluid to the floor. 'Only joking,' he said, looking at me with laughing eyes.

I stared back, puzzled and very amused.

With a, 'Mind if I take a peek?' he began to investigate my toiletry bags. 'Now that's nice, mmm. I can see we're not going to have any trouble keeping you smelling beautiful. Now look at this, what a fantastic colour is that!' He delved deeper into the small bags, unearthing sweet scents, talcs and make-up which I now rarely used. Abruptly, he stood up and said it was time to prepare to meet the team of doctors and associates. They'd probably need to look at my legs, and then he'd dress them again.

'And what are you going to dress them in?'

'Oh, a nice little Armani bandage would look good, don't you think?' and he was gone.

This banter occurred whenever Paul nursed me, which was often. The limb surgery ward was a specialist unit, with nursing staff trained to deal with amputees. Paul was one of the very best – a godsend. He healed patients' spirits as much as the treatments and drugs he had to hand out on a daily basis.

The "team" arrived. Mr Robinson, my consultant orthopaedic surgeon, was flanked by house-doctors, nurses, social welfarers, prosthetists and physiotherapists, or physioterrorists as I called them.

A sombre, self-effacing man, Mr Robinson didn't crack his face to a smile once. Fake or otherwise. Not even with my drug induced jokes which were my way of handling being gawped at by the crowd of twelve people who filled my room every morning. I learned later of his skills as a surgeon. He'd been one of the people to deal with the horrific injuries that occurred at the Clapham Junction railway disaster, called out to amputate on the spot. I respected him, but boy did I want to get him to laugh, or even smile.

He asked if I'd seen the injuries. I shook my head with disdainful horror at the thought. A gas and air tank was brought in to help with the pain of having the dressings opened up. It wasn't enough, so was topped up with yet more narcotics. I began singing the *Porgy and Bess* song *Summertime* at the top of my voice. I discovered singing to be a great breathing exercise and it helped me to endure pain. In St. George's I had made up little songs which went something like:

Diana went up the hill, aha aha
Diana went up the hill aha
Her hair was long, her legs had gone
But bloody hell her arms were strong

The consultant's prognosis was not good. The above knee amputation on the left was fine and healing well, but my below knee leg was not suitable in its ripped state for the prospect of a false limb fitting. More operations were required, and possibly plastic surgery. I experienced twinges of fear at the thought of this, but put them on the back burner whilst I adapted to my new surroundings and absorbed the legal situation that was developing by the day.

Steve Hampshire had notified BR that we intended to sue. We would apply for a split trial. Hopefully getting a trial on liability in the Spring. Quantum, the measure of damages to be awarded, would be dealt with the following year if we were successful on the question of liability.

Studying the evidence so far, he noticed that WPC John's report was dated 13th August. The first newspaper article hadn't appeared until the l6th, and he knew we'd done nothing up until the paper came out. The official witness statements (ie the driver and the guard) were taken by British Transport Police on 17th August, just the day after BR told the press they were going to sue me.

The next we heard was that Steve's partner Christopher Johnson had interviewed WPC Johns. Paddy's recommendation was coming good, it appeared we had the crucial crack team of lawyers we so desperately needed.

I read their report over and over again.

WPC Johns' evidence as a witness was weak. She didn't arrive on the scene until 10 minutes after the accident and her report was based on her talking to the train guard who'd "seen it happen". He'd seen me run to "get on the train as it moved away".

The hunt for other passengers on the train, including the crucial witness we'd found and lost, continued. The paramedics, the taxi drivers in the station taxi rank, and angel Maggie Hammond were all interviewed.

Towards the end of August, Helen got an article in the press requesting witnesses, and Debbie Crammond got in touch.

Debbie had been on the train reading the paper at the time. She hadn't seen me fall but she clearly remembered the black man. She'd seen him right by the accident, shaken to bits. She also noticed that they'd been at the station for quite a long time when the train moved off with a judder. Then she heard the screaming. When asked if this was before or after the train moved she replied that it was after. She also remembered four children on the platform, two boys and two girls. Maggie didn't see it happen either but she'd heard the screaming from the next set of stairs at the station. She couldn't say if she'd heard the train move and then a scream or a scream and then the train. She described how she'd knelt down and held my hand. Apparently I was unbelievably lucid. I'd told her that an ambulance was on its way and had asked her her name.

Maggie's friends John and Kate Lowe had called to the ticket collector to call an ambulance as they ran past and down to me on the platform, but when they ran up the stairs again he still hadn't left his post to call an ambulance. He suggested they ask someone at the main entrance.

They ran to the ticket office and got the lady there to dial 999. Whilst they waited for the paramedics to arrive, she had gone down to the platform, returning with some crass remark like "silly girl, tried to get on the train when it was moving". Which they then thought is what must have happened.

Kate and Maggie stayed with me the whole time, trying to reassure me. The only BR staff they remembered were the ones who talked to the ambulance crew about the electricity. John reckoned there must have been about 20 people on the platform when the ambulance arrived. That's when he noticed the four kids. He didn't know where they'd come from but they were there for a long time.

Maggie then described how they got the train off me. It was risky apparently because they had to turn the electricity back on to move the train. It took about forty minutes to get me into the ambulance.

John had noticed the great distance between the bottom of the stairs where I'd tried to board and the place where I'd finally fallen. Nobody had been asked for a statement. John had actually volunteered. He'd got as far as giving his name and address but when he said he'd only heard and not seen the accident, the BR official didn't want any more details from him. He was there when the guard gave his evidence, remembering it clearly because, he said, it was so brief and off-hand for such a serious incident. The guard spoke first saying, 'I saw her go under and I pulled the cord.' The guard didn't mention if the train was moving or not and the driver had apparently nodded and said, 'When that happened, then I stopped the train.'

"...saw her go under." "...then I stopped the train."

Those two sentences were heavily underlined by Christopher Johnson, with a note at the end saying John was pretty much sure he'd remembered word for word what had been said.

At the end of August the Area Manager of British Rail had then phoned Coopers to say he'd spoken to various people involved, including their own solicitors, who were of the view that British Rail should be seen to be taking the initiative. So, they said they'd be prepared to put a board up on the station asking for witnesses to get in touch. With THEM. Once BR's solicitors had contacted any witnesses they would then pass on any information to Coopers.

As if!

What guarantee, Coopers enquired, would they have that BR would pass on any information other than that which suited them? What was the reason behind it? To which the Area Manager replied 'pass'! He then repeated his question and got the response 'that is the way our solicitors feel we should play it.'

'What is the problem?' he said. 'Our solicitors are honorable people.'

He was, said Christopher, totally unconcerned about the unfairness of the situation.

Of course, because it was British Rail's property, we had no come-back on this but had to go along with their suggestions.

CHAPTER TWELVE

Hello And Goodbye

I gradually became immersed in the hospital regime.

Woken at 6am for a cup of tea, medication, changing of drips. Fall asleep for an hour. Woken by two nurses to get me ready for the ward round. Bed bath, hair brush, perfume, bit of make-up if feeling just slightly energetic. Looked at by usual crowd of twelve filling my room, muttering medical phrases that meant nothing to me. Watch some television. Tick off lunch and dinner menus for next day. Dressing changed. Visitors.

Lovely wonderful visitors continued to flow in, as did the flowers, cards and letters. Even the two amazing ambulance men who had rescued me from under the train sent in a massive bunch of flowers. I heard much later that they had delivered this floral kindness partly out of relief that I had lived. Neither believed that I could have survived. By now I'd become more discerning over who I really wanted to see. I had to filter out the accident freaks, the rubber-necker type who like to set up camp next to motorway accidents and crack open the Thermos and sandwiches. These were the strangest band of people. Acquaintances, people I barely knew, who for some reason had a bizarre thirst to be close to tragedy. I couldn't hack it. I needed people who'd be helpful if required, who'd chat away but would stop to listen to me if I was keen to talk.

I certainly had my favourites, those who'd make my day a better one. Among these were Dinah and Annie, actors who I'd met on my days on *Brookside*, the Channel 4 soap opera; journalist mates Christine, Jane, Barbie and Chris, Angus and Julian, and many others I had worked with. I was eternally thankful that I'd made such good friends in the past. They were now supporting me with courage for the future.

I never asked Andrew to visit. I was still, ironically, playing hard to get, a pattern I couldn't relinquish even in my sedentary hopelessly dependent position. But I needed him around desperately, a disturbing emotion that sometimes bordered on panic. He came in frequently with hugs and kisses, settling himself down at the bottom of my bed where my goodies were stashed. There he ate his way through boxes of chocolates and biscuits, smacking his lips with a vengeance for comfort.

A week after entering Roehampton, staff sister Jackie allowed me to go out in a car with a crowd of friends that included Andrew, Helen and Duncan.

Boosted with a jab of Diamorphine, I gingerly slipped from the wheelchair into the front passenger seat of Helen's car. My body shook with the effort. I wore a long blue skirt and a little bodice top I'd nicked from Dinah earlier in the week. It was peculiar to be in a car. I didn't recognise roads as roads, more as wide spaces that made my guts churn with terror. Like a child, everything seemed too big and overpowering. I felt tiny in mind, body and spirit.

I also felt an intense mourning of loss for my connection with the earth. This came as a shock. Something that's taken wholly for granted is the job of connecting to the ground that feet carry out. I'd lost it and felt, still feel, a literal sense of being adrift, of airborne loss.

We went to a pub. As I moved to get out of the car, I had the disturbing experience of attempting to swivel as I moved to stand out of the car. The phantom legs, the ghosts of the legs now dead, did the total action for me, so I found myself attempting to stand in space. It was only Helen yelling my name that brought my concentration back to the present. All the energy that the legs had produced in their lifetime was still, somehow, hanging around.

The phenomenon called "phantom pain" still isn't fully understood. There was one particular event that haunts me to this day. I was sitting outside in the wheelchair, enjoying the company of a couple of MediaVision clients, old friends from *Brookside* who had set up their own independent production company. Thinking I'd heard Andrew's motorbike, I turned my head to look right away into the distance at the car park. I suddenly felt sick beyond belief. My brain registered "someone is standing in my legs". I turned back and there was Colin, smiling and leaning towards me to give me a kiss, standing exactly where my legs should have been. 'Get away! Stop standing in my legs!' I shrieked in shock.

A logical explanation would be that the brain thinks something is very wrong, and so still sends out nerve impulses. And yet this does not explain the type of phantom pain I still experience now, where my "previous" body still walks for me. If you turn your attention to the soles of your feet as you read this, you'll feel a kind of presence, a tingling. I feel that too. Sometimes too much.

There are triggers that can bring the phantoms on: if I'm upset and emotional or if there's a change in the weather, especially if it's freezing cold. Most notably, strong electromagnetic fields can cause the phantoms to become torturous. Sometimes I get the feeling that my right leg is on back to front. That's how it was left on the train track. I've felt my feet on back to front, and sometimes I feel something pulling my toenails out one by one.

I rationalise this to myself with the thought that I had the legs for 29 years, and it will take a further 29 years in my new body to come to terms with itself physically. These strange phenomena have certainly made me feel less sceptical about "otherworldly" energy forces.

Andrew lifted me out and into the wheelchair. He pushed me over bumps in the grass which made me wince and we settled beside a plastic table. I watched people drinking and laughing from a distance. It was so good to be out in the fresh air, yet this was not a world that I could relate to in any shape or form.

I was the proverbial fish out of water, a mermaid on dry land.

Andrew was openly affectionate and I wanted him to stay near to me. He seemed extra manly and strong and I felt I could rely on him. The painkiller began to wear off and I needed to get back to the hospital quickly. My legs, or "leggies" as I called them, began to shake and vibrate as a response to the fear I began to feel at being outside, away from bed. The small territory I could relate to.

I was rushed back. Once safely installed, Andrew lay on the bed with me. We kissed. I was beginning to fall totally in love with him. A love born of need, of an emotional craving for a link with the outside world. But a love no less real for that. I stroked his black shiny hair and admired and loved his beautiful face. As I stroked him it filled me with pleasure, as if someone were softly caressing me. I remembered all the good things we'd done before the accident. Horse-riding, enjoying a drink, snogging our way round Soho and a group of lads we'd passed singing a love song at us with drunken voices.

I craved with all my heart and soul to return to that world. It was, at times, all I could think of. My life previous to the accident had taken on a magical quality. There was only good in the past. I sensed the bond that had been developing between us was getting stronger.

'Do you realise how much people love you, Di?' he said. I flowered at his words, the nearest he'd got to being emotional. Still though, we couldn't talk about the future.

After nearly two weeks of adjusting, I was told I was ready for the first stage of my rehabilitation: mobility on wheels. I was to leave my bed under my own steam.

Nurse Alison and I had a little argument over my catheter, which had been in since I'd arrived. I'd been free to drink water and juices to my heart's content and now she wanted to remove the tube. I glared sulkily at the wheelchair which had been placed beside my bed, looking as strange and alien as a Dalek from *Doctor Who*. I didn't fancy the anguish of having to ask for the bed-pan continually – yet another thing to worry about. She won, of course, and I hauled myself up very carefully from the flat of the bed into the wheelchair. I rolled slowly out of the room and down the long gloss-surfaced corridor.

A theatre bed was being pushed out of a room near mine. I stopped. On the bed was a small hunched figure lying under the white sheets with a pink shower cap on its head. The head turned and a goatee bearded face greeted me with a wide smile.

'Good'ay, I'm Brett.'

'Hi,' I nodded. 'Diana. Are you going for surgery?'

'Fraid so. Still, it's nice to see a pretty face before I go under. As they say.'

'Thanks.' I brushed the hair back from my face. 'Best of luck. I'm thinking of you.' I felt only the deepest empathy for someone who was facing the dreadful push down to theatre.

I began to move away, and called, 'I like your cap Brett.'

'Thanks darling. Say, when I come round from the oppo, how's about I get me best leg over?'

I giggled my way to the recreation room where I found Nurse Paul with other assorted people, all in wheelchairs. They looked so strange. Yet I knew I looked like them: a trunk of body with large bits of leg missing. Most had lost one leg. I had to acknowledge then that I was likely to be the worst off one of the lot of us.

I looked down at the chasm below my left thigh and right knee. It was incomprehensible and still not at all real. Part of me wholly believed that somehow God would wake me up from this nightmare. I had to believe that.

Nurse Paul gave me a quick hug, 'You can meet them all later, Di,' he whispered and pushed me back to my room.

A sense of loss fell over me. Shallow or not, looks had been important to me and my mourning for my severe loss of sexual power ran in close parallel to my more practical losses. I'd been at my most potent. A 29 year old leggy brunette, living in the most exciting city in the world going places with my own rapidly expanding company.

In my single days I'd found myself in situations with some very powerful men other than Max, and quite a few of them had made plays for me. Some were persistent in their desire to make me another notch on their bedposts, but I never gave in. I'd always called the shots in relationships. I always wanted to be the woman who said no. And, apart from Max, I did. Thriving on my unattainability.

There was a large trestle table out on the limb surgery ward where some twelve people would go to eat. Not well enough to join them, I remained in my room, ordering food that was never eaten. The mass doses of antibiotics and drugs had cut my appetite to nothing. I was losing weight at a rate that was worrying to everyone except me. My stomach was concave, and, when I dared to look down as they changed the dressings, I could see that what was left of my legs were like sticks, bony with little flesh. I didn't look at the actual injuries, but I wished that I was more symmetrical and wished that the surgeons would chop off my right knee so that my legs were at least the same size.

Sarah came in almost daily, bringing, at my request, work. We wrote proposals together, she brought my small Amstrad PC and I tried to get my brain to work. It was difficult, the continual distractions of routine were many. I was waiting for the next chunk of news from Coopers. Every communication from them came with a nag that I simply had to get on with writing my statement. I hadn't been able to face it and didn't know how I was going to face it. I felt so distanced from the world outside, and, without realizing, was becoming institutionalised. I got on with the routine. I greeted visitors with big smiles and jokes and endless chatter. Alone in the silent darkness was my only time and space for grieving alone. I cried nearly every night I was in hospital and I was there for over five months.

Even sleep at that time, when it came, had its own horrors. I started having a recurring dream about a train, an old-fashioned Western train with open doors and running boards. I was standing a little way away, watching it roll by. A girl would appear on the running board, her long, flowing hair, rippling in the breeze. She wore a yellow mini skirt and had one arm raised, waving and smiling at me. The girl was me. I was waving myself goodbye.

CHAPTER THIRTEEN

How Come U Don't Call Me Any More?

As another operation, for something called debridement and degloving, approached, my fear, and my need for Andrew, increased. Ever since I had signed the first, sinister, operation consent form I wholly believed that I'd been fated to die on the railway track and that each operation was going to finally do the job properly and finish me off.

I guess at this stage I'd become mentally dependent on Andrew – I wasn't aware of the role the morphine-based, love-inducing, drugs were playing at the time. I'd noticed that Andrew seemed to feel closer to me if I showed dependence, so I decided to change tack and ask for his help. Would he see me into the theatre ante-room? He conceded, but with the comment, 'I've missed a lot of work already.'

It hurt, but I let it go. His parents were due to visit from Germany and arrangements had been made for them to come in to meet me. This had to be a Good Sign, pointing loud and clear to our future together. I couldn't help thinking, though, what a rotten kind of introduction to a possible future daughter-in-law, the mother of their grandchildren, it would be.

Before all of that I had to get through the operation. Gulping slightly with trepidation himself, Andrew held my hand down the corridor of death leading to the ante-room. I felt better with him at my side. As usual the pre-med hadn't calmed me, I needed him there to assuage the terror which left me almost breathless with fright.

The general anaesthetics put me into a mysterious twilight zone, a state of being where I didn't exist. My blood chilled at the thought of what the surgeons had had to do in that first big operation I'd erroneously witnessed. They'd used drills, knives and the theatre had been filled with the sound of bone being sawed. What did debridement mean? (No internet then – thank goodness.) What knives would Mr Robinson be using? How bright was that theatre light? It was cold, clinical and frightening beyond measure.

These thoughts filled my head along with the one that at least if I had Andrew there his face would be the last one I would see. But it was not to be. He let go of my hand in the corridor and slipped away before we got to the ante-room. Alone, I had to concentrate on good thoughts as they put me under.

When I woke up back in my room, Andrew wasn't there. Instead, Mum and Helen were at the bottom of my bed, scrabbling among the various hampers of delights that I'd been sent.

'Where's Andrew?'

'He's only just gone. He fell asleep waiting for you to come round.'

'He said he'd be here. And STOP eating all MY food, will you?' I snapped. Lost to irritable pain, I couldn't see why, if I wasn't eating it, someone else should.

'We're not,' said Mum, her little mouth full of chocolate.

They attempted to soothe me but the pain was scorching its way around my legs, especially in the areas where my legs no longer existed. I was cranky and distressed and couldn't see that they too needed comfort – in their case from food. There was so much there. Duncan had even cooked a wonderful lobster dish and brought it in – eaten with relish by the lucky visitors on shift that night.

'Why didn't Andrew stay?'

'He did, but he wasn't coping with the long wait, Di. I just looked at that lovely face of his and suggested he went and got some proper rest. His parents are arriving tomorrow.'

'Tell me about it.'

'Blame me if you want. Is he alright, Di? I think he needs to talk to someone. Helen and I are counselling each other. He spoke of someone called Janine.'

Janine – the fiancée who dumped him at the altar. This revved up my crankiness beyond belief.

'Do you suppose he's thinking of that grief as well now?' continued my dear, ever-concerned mum.

I was boiling inside but managed to dismiss her sensible comments with a shrug and an irritated bark. 'I don't want to talk about it.'

'Ask for strength my darling baby girl,' she replied softly. 'And it shall come.'

CHAPTER FOURTEEN

Everybody's Got To Learn Sometime

Andrew's parents came in the day after my operation. Still weak, I managed to make up my face and do my hair. I did my best to seem pleasant and pain-free but I probably talked too much. Andrew's dad sat opposite and didn't say a word. His mum barely spoke to me either. She couldn't take her eyes from Andrew.

'Dad hates hospitals,' he said defensively after they'd gone.

Who the hell doesn't! I wanted to yell. Instead, in a continuation of the close policing of my "meet the relatives" behaviour, I paused and took a breath.

'He's a child psychiatrist,' I said calm as anything. 'You'd think he'd be used to them. Everyone hates hospitals.'

I couldn't keep up the ridiculous pantomime. It had been dreadful, I sobbed. What a way to meet his parents for the first time.

'Hey, come on,' he said gruffly, putting his arms around me. Realising my tactic of needing him had failed I'd quickly reverted back to independent mode. So instead of feeling comforted, I was cursing the fact that I now needed him so badly. All the same, I clung to him because it felt so good to be cuddled.

After he'd gone, his mum phoned my new mobile, an early Dom Joly comedy-sized model with the weight of a brick, given to me by a dear friend.

'Could I speak to Andrew please?' she said. And then added, as if an afterthought, 'How long will you be in do you think?'

'Difficult to say,' I said breezily, best behaviour back in place. 'I need to learn to walk again. Another couple of months probably.'

I sensed she was making more than a mental note of this. Not sounding at all like a future mother-in-law, she wished me well.

This behaviour resonated disturbingly with my most-recurring fantasy. The narcotics made me sleepy, dreamy and at times extremely relaxed. They also made me feel sexually aroused. I couldn't fantasise about having sex as I couldn't begin to imagine what it would be like for me now, without legs. What I could picture, in full 3D vivid colour no less, thanks to the hallucinogenic properties of my daily drug cocktails, was my future wedding.

Mid-morning when the drugs were having their most sedating effect, I craved sleep. Sleep, I was to discover, would be the best healer of all but at this time of day it nearly always eluded me. So instead I'd drift into this full-on wedding day scene. I'd see myself walking, standing tall and dressed in an ivory creation, my hair bedecked in purple flowers. I was able to see with my own eyes the gorgeous colours, the smiling, the beauty of everything around me and yet I could never put Andrew in the picture. The groom was there all right. At the altar, patiently waiting for me in his black tails, but he was always standing with his back to me so I could never see his face.

Just before I reached the altar, as he moved to turn round to greet me with that special groom's smile, the druggy haze would suddenly lift, rocketing me sharply back into the chill, bleak reality of my surroundings: hospital as home, a world away from the flower-filled church of beauty, health and happiness. Back to the pain, the worries about my future life as a disabled person and the uncertainties about Andrew's love for me. Most difficult of all, trying to come to terms with the highly public accusation that I'd put myself into this position. That I wasn't a victim, I was an *offender*. That this was all my fault. That I was supposed to think myself lucky I wasn't being sued for trespass. All of it, every single bit of it, was beyond belief. It had to be a continuation of dream turned to nightmare. Had to be.

Solicitor Steve Hampshire wanted to come in and see me again. I tried to put him off. The last thing I needed was pressure to write the dreaded statement. I knew it was important, crucial, but I also knew my own strengths. Walking School was looming and my health had to come first. But he was insistent, dangling the carrot that he had some good news. Even knowing the dryness of lawyers who don't tend to bandy around joyous statements which they can't deliver on, I was sceptical. But eventually I agreed. Allowing him to bring with him the witness statements gathered so far but with no guarantee as to when I'd be able to face reading them.

Steve's news was good. Very good. They'd secured the services of Stan Hall, British Rail's safety expert for over ten years and the author of several seminal books on railway safety practices with titles such as *Danger On The Line, Danger Signals* and *History of Railway Inspectorate*. Titles I would have found as dry as ditchwater in another life. Titles which now lifted my spirits to the roof.

I listened attentively as Steve filled me in. Stan is surprised at the actions, or rather non-actions, of the operating superintendent on duty that day. He's shocked that there hasn't been a public enquiry, let alone an internal one. News would have reached the superintendent on the evening of the accident. If nothing else he should then have ordered an immediate enquiry to ensure that the train was safe. For all he knew the accident could have been fatal. If nothing at all else, the brakes of the train should have been checked, safety procedures should have been followed, and measurements of the debris positions should have been taken on the day of the accident. Stan couldn't believe that none of this had been done.

BR's response to Stan's questions, put to them by Steve, was that their staff had followed safety procedures and stopped the train and all the blame was mine. Therefore they didn't need to hold an enquiry. Stan agreed with our own suspicions that their tardy behaviour and responses could well be tied in to BR's rising push for profitability, especially with the government pushing harder than ever for privatisation.

We learnt the inside BR gossip from Stan. Safety standards had plummeted. After the Purley rail crash in March 1989 a driver had been jailed for criminal negligence. Our driver and guard would have been aware of that. As they wouldn't have been aware of whether I was going to live or die. Saying I got on a moving train would seem to be the most convenient way of explaining away any safety breach. Cover-up or incompetence, Stan said we had to now prove I'd boarded a stationary train.

I was more than ready for this. Ready with all of my being to let the world know that I had been telling the truth. Heart pounding, I asked Steve for the statements and settled down to read with my mind on full-alert. Reading and re-reading, writing and rewriting, is part of my job and I do it well. I picked out a few important points I wanted Cooper's to address.

How long was it before Mr & Mrs Lowe decided to turn around and retrace their steps when they heard my screaming? I think it's important that Mr Lowe could hear the train moving and my screaming concurrently. So we need to find out how long it takes for a train to move from the stairs to where I ended up and how long I was alongside the train before being dragged under. Timing is crucial. The time it took them to stop the train will show if they were doing their job. The rules say the guard is supposed to see the train safely out of the station. If he was watching why didn't he stop the train sooner?

Mr Lowe says he heard the guard say 'I saw her go under and I pulled the cord'. So he was watching me being dragged along and did nothing?

In their statements both the driver and the guard say the train moved off "at about 18.29". Aren't they supposed to know exactly? And the fact that they both use the same phrase – isn't that evidence of collusion?

Steve thinks this is because the station manager wrote both statements as told to him at the time.

Even more reason to think it's an "official" version.

CHAPTER FIFTEEN

Falling

'If you're well enough to go to the pub, you are well enough to eat meals with the rest of the patients and join in the meetings,' Ward Sister Jackie snapped when I had again asked to eat in my room.

I was feeling isolated but I didn't want to play the institutional game. Gradually they wore me down and I was forced from my lair. I was still painfully thin and it was hoped that I would eat more if I went out for meals, as it were, rather than staying in on my own.

By this time I'd become firm friends with my pal from the op trolley I'd met on my first foray into the corridors of Queen Mary's. We were the only other trauma patients (as sudden accident victims are known) on the ward. Brett had lost one leg below the knee after a motorbike accident. He'd been a scaffolder and shared the same doubts and fears about a life that had suddenly been ripped away and would now be so different. Though I don't think there are many scaffolders who are ever short of a swear word or two, I'm sure Brett, too, found swearing a great release from his post-traumatic stress syndrome. Our conversations were liberally decorated as we effed and blinded our way around the ward and the coffee shop together. This, I would later learn, was the kind of close, intense bonding that happens to soldiers on battlefields where normal life, life "outside" the situation, has ceased to exist.

We laughed at each other, with each other, and at ourselves a lot. I really enjoyed this new accursed side of my personality coming out. There were joke competitions and I would raid my visitors' brains for new funny tales from the outside.

Brett and I were the youngsters around the communal lunchtime ward table and, operations aside and energy permitting, we'd play up. What with our cussing double-act alongside Senile Edith, Group Captain David,

Good-Mannered Tom, Robber Ray, Cathy The One Legged Witch (because of her wild hair and rambling conversation), all MC'd by a masterful Camp Nurse Paul, most mealtimes disintegrated into a Cuckoo's Nest farce of humour and surrealism.

The majority of patients were victims of diabetes, and, through loss of circulation and then feeling, their limbs would become severely ulcerated and have to be amputated. One man who had actually chosen to have an amputation was Ray, a cheerful cockney who'd suffered an industrial accident leaving his left hand totally without feeling and useless. In hope that he would get more use from a false hand up to the elbow he'd courageously decided to have the arm amputated.

'It's God's way of getting 'is own back Di,' he explained one day over the table. 'I bin a robber most of me life. Only robbed the rich, mind, but still, soon as I get meself a proper job, nearly lose the bloody arm, don't I?' Refusing all painkillers, he was jogging a couple of hours after his amputation. 'It's taking the piss, Di. Couldn't feel a thing when the useless bloody arm was there. Now it's gone I can feel everyfink!'

Edith was nearly 80 in age, a white haired lady who'd clearly been a beauty and still retained a dignified air   until it was time to eat. Every mealtime her head would gradually sink by degrees until, without fail, her face would end up in her uneaten meal. We discovered that it was her medication. She'd become slightly senile and if left unmedicated for too long would bite and kick with her one good leg before gradually fading away. She took it on herself to start smoking again, having asked Brett and I many questions as to what it was like. She was moved some months later because she managed to sneak a ciggy in her room. When she was discovered by Wing Commander David, she tried to put it out with tissues and set fire to the bedclothes.

David, the Wing-Commander, or Group Captain, was so-called because he'd frequently hark back to World War Two and the part he played, barking out orders to Paul and the other nurses with the forceful attitude of a Sergeant Major in Barracks.

'Water please,' then a slap of his hand on the table. 'Half a cup of black coffee, no sugar.' His 'Pass me the mustard' became a secret catch-phrase between Nurse Paul, Brett and I. Paul would always retain his temper admirably, getting his own back with his quaint, Julian Clary-style humour.

One day a few of us were sitting outside for a glorious flypast of Second World War aeroplanes, a celebration for the Battle of Britain, when

David, in his wheelchair, saluted and wiped a tear from his eye. I was deeply moved. He'd so wanted to stand in proper acknowledgement.

I recognised in my more lucid moments that to cope with the trauma, both mental and physical, I was going to have to reinvent myself. To dig very deeply into the strengths of the old Diana to help cope with the new one. I concentrated on humour and sensitivity and a natural sense of the bizarre. This often led to comments like, 'I didn't like my legs anyway.' 'I was always too tall.' 'Now I'll be able to have really slim ankles.'

The humour kept the real issues at bay because I couldn't deal with them. Much was down to body image, first mentioned by my surgeon Mr Robinson, a phrase I'd not come across until then. This was my view for the outside world. A view still peppered with arrogance and a bit of vanity whereas the real new Diana was the one I began to work on. This involved scratching into my soul, talking with it. Asking it questions. Willing it on. A form of meditation calling out in silence to my innermost being to give me the strength to get through it.

The problem was I could see no end to these troubles. It wasn't like I was going to get "better". So, paradoxically, as I became as "better" as I was ever going to become, the irreversibility of my situation began to encroach on my natural optimism. Unable to cope with the fact that I would never see my legs again, I kept searching for reasons. I made lists. Lists in my mind of reasons for the accident.

1. It was an accident. Stupid, senseless and with no meaning.
2. It had happened because God had chosen me for a purpose. I was closer to Jesus through suffering and had been brought back to life by God to show his love.
3. It was a battle of good vs evil and evil forces had created the accident.
4. My life had become superficial and without meaning. Meaning had to be forced back into my life. I'd been on the wrong road and I needed a road that led somewhere different than the track I had been on.
5. My spirit had lived other lives. When we die we go somewhere and learn everything we have been searching for. We choose to return to the earth as another spirit, but with some of the knowledge retained from our previous souls or spirits. I was an old spirit and had been sent with advance strength to withstand such an incident.
6. A statistic.

It hadn't helped that they'd started letting me out of the hospital more and more. Venturing into all that "outside" beyond the hospital grounds was a major challenge. I never knew what in the world was going to suddenly rear up into my face and slap me next. My first social situation, the wedding of Andrew's best friends, Susan and John, turned out to be a painful occasion. The impact of seeing me newly (to them) disabled and in a wheelchair was a shock that many couldn't disguise. It was nigh impossible for me to interact in any normal sense at all.

John cried throughout his speech, and I had to withstand the first of many facile comments such as, 'So sorry about what happened.' 'You've still got a nice face though, haven't you?' 'Have you got brothers? Sisters? Perhaps they will have children and then you can be an auntie.'

I was becoming "public property". Some folk thought it was OK to comment on my visible differences however crass their questions and statements. (For the record, it wasn't and it isn't.)

I wore a very long skirt to cover all the bandages but it kept getting caught up in the wheelchair wheels. Andrew had to push me around. A bit like a new mum with their first pram, he struggled and sweated to get me through inaccessible doorways. Having to sit in the conservatory away from the main wedding party didn't help either. I tried to appear cheerful but inside I was screaming with grief. It was a relief to return to my friends and the insane humour back inside the hospital.

We were all sitting out in the sunshine one day watching Ray practise with his new false arm. In an attempt to trim the bushes that surrounded the tiny patch of garden next to the ward, he brandished a pair of secateurs. A lady was walking across the car-park when she slipped. To stop herself falling completely, she tried to balance herself with her hands in an awkward position on the ground. Ray and I had been watching this with amusement when he slipped off his falsie and threw it into her path.

'Here you are love,' he yelled. 'I'll give you a hand.'

She paled with shock and I tried not to scream with laughter. I don't know why it was, and is, so funny to watch other people fall over. I suppose it's because I've been through my fair share of fallings. And was about to do so again.

CHAPTER SIXTEEN

Once In A Lifetime

I was collected for my first day of Walking School by Nurse Lovie Lottie.

'Are you alright, Love? Soon be better, Love. Going to be walking today, Love?' she wittered on as she wheeled me through the grey, damp, rainy gardens to the large gymnasium-like building in the hospital grounds.

With the obligatory 'See you later, Love,' she parked me inside the high-roofed, echoing hall and vanished. Struck dumb, I didn't even have time to thank her.

I couldn't believe the scene before me. A living nightmare that even Hieronymus Bosch would have had difficulty believing. My only way of absorbing it was to think that it couldn't possibly be real. That it was another drug-induced nightmare that God was going to wake me from at any moment.

My eyes fixed onto a man the size of an eight-year-old child walking between parallel bars. His body was average human height but he'd lost both legs above the knee and was walking on a tiny pair of practise legs. I realised I'd been taken there to be a part of it.

Were they going to make *me* do that?

No way. No effing way.

Everywhere I looked that first day there were humiliating sights far removed from normal human experience. Tap tap tap. Crashes to the ground. Cries of pain bouncing off the echoing roof. People walking up and down rows of bars, with sticks, in wheelchairs, all with metal or wooden legs.

'This isn't me,' I whimpered into the white coat of a physiotherapist. 'I must be in a nightmare. I must wake up.'

The head of the physioterrorist team, as Brett and I had christened them, was a bolshie, practical woman with a no-nonsense manner called Penny. She personally wheeled me back to the ward.

'This isn't me,' I repeated.

I'd said that under the train too. Why couldn't I wake myself up out of this?

Penny sat on my bed and explained what I had to do. How I'd need courage but that they knew I could do it. With immaculate timing, Todd, the prosthetist assigned to my case, brought in a false leg and showed me how it worked. It was alien but, like the wheelchair, I had to force myself to understand that this was what I needed to adjust to. If I wanted to walk again I'd have to make a start in getting used to it.

These people aren't known as the world experts for nothing. They're trained to teach trauma-management holistically with all its attendant psychological, social and fiscal challenges. With Penny's scarily stern but strangely gentle encouragement and Todd's reassuring presence, I thought of Andrew and willed myself to think of the future, of walking beside him.

The following day, a full month exactly since the accident, I stood for the first time. It involved putting both stumps into blue inflatable pylons and being raised, as slowly as a shipwreck, by four people. Immediately I felt dizzy but relished looking at my helpers in the eye. I clung to the bars, sweat dripped from every pore, but still I remained standing.

'I'm a giraffe!' I smiled.

'Now you know that we'll have to make you slightly shorter than your original height, don't you?' said Todd. 'Somewhere around the five foot six mark?' He studied my face for a reaction.

'Mr Robinson did mention it, yes.' I paused. 'But you're not going to are you Todd?'

'If you want to walk unaided by sticks...'

'But I was five foot ten inches tall, and that's what I want to be now.'

'It's the balance, Diana. It will be too difficult.'

Balance is all. Douglas Bader, who had exactly the same injuries as me, walked unaided everywhere but he was a short man whose prosthetic legs were made slightly smaller. It took a lot of arguing but I persisted. Body image was beginning to mean a great deal to me. I couldn't go from being a tall girl to a short girl. It would never be me. On top of which I am blessed with very good balance – I was a dancer, a horse rider – I must at least be allowed to try to be my old self. I sensed Todd's argument weakening.

'I'll do it if you do,' was my last word on the matter, grinning with effort.

From that day on an almost super-human effort was involved. It's impossible to imagine what it's like to lose your legs. I can only relay, from an energy point of view, how my consultant surgeon explained the effort of walking on false legs. Bi-lateral amputees use up to 180% additional energies when walking. Every step taken is the equivalent to an able bodied person walking every comparative step up a very severe incline or hill. In the early days, add in extreme pain.

I awoke the following day unable to face walking school. Just the sight of a prosthetic leg was too distressing for me. Without any pleading I was allowed to stay in bed all day. As I tried to deal with the next emotional stage of the feelings of loss for my legs, I realised for the first time that my left leg had been burnt off at the time of the accident. I couldn't get the image out of my mind but I wasn't allowed another day off "school".

Whilst my right leg was fitted with a simple prosthetic to help me stand, my left leg had what's known as a PPAM, a Pneumatic Post-Amputation Mobility Aid, a metal frame attached to an inflatable bag.

At first I learnt to stand, holding onto the parallel bars for two or three minutes or so. Balance was extremely difficult and I'd get terrible vertigo. But I had to prove to Todd, if nobody else, that I could do it.

Stepping out with my stronger, right, leg first, I set off between the parallel bars. I felt so high up! To the shouts of 'go on Di, you can do it!' from my physios, I walked up and down ten times. I collapsed back into my wheelchair, exhausted but jubilant, anxious to find Brett so that I could celebrate my achievement over a well-earned drink or two.

Before I could have my own pair of legs made I had to endure another operation, to save and secure my only knee. Part of the procedure was to have photos taken of my injuries, giving the surgeons clearer dimensions of the work to be done. That particular morning, stripped of all dignity and dressings, I lay on the bed, ready to be covered in the brown iodine that was also part of the pre-op procedure. There was a curt tap at the door and it was flung open. A lanky boy, cameras swinging round his neck, strutted in.

'Come to do the photos,' he announced, picking at a boil on his face. I felt that someone, a nurse should have been there, but before I could explain, he had pulled off the cage over my legs and began to look.

'Ooh nasty. Accident was it?'

Too shocked to speak, I nodded my head.

'You're going to plastic surgery today?' He pulled up a camera and started to angle it towards me. 'You'll be having the cheese grater then.'

'The *what*?' I replied, bile rising in my throat, wanting to tell him to piss off.

'It's like a cheese grater, they scrape a thick layer of skin off – probably your thigh or stomach. Scrapings of skin like cheese. Hurts like hell afterwards.'

The flash went off and I froze with trepidation.

'Get out. Get *out* of my room.'

He took another photo and left. Later, I made an official complaint, but the tunnel of fear down into the theatre world became an even more dreadful journey.

Alison and another lovely nurse Mary came with me. We had to wait in the corridor and I clung on to Alison's hand, my heart thumping with fear. All I could think about was the cheese grater.

'I'm going to die,' I whispered to Alison.

'Now now pet, you'll be OK.'

I was OK. In fact I felt that the delicate operation of removing a large piece of skin from my thigh, some of which was put onto the end of my right leg, seemed promising. I ran no fever and within ten days Mr Robinson said the skin graft had taken well.

I'd been so unwell for such a long time, with every small piece of good news I felt a new rallying surge of determination. This had started back in intensive care, when, as they moved me out into a ward room, I realised I wasn't dead yet. It was like my body speaking to me – let's get out of here. It was almost miraculous.

CHAPTER SEVENTEEN

Rehab

The first sight of my training legs was a shock. I had to face the reality that these ugly metal things were going to be part of me and let them strap them to my body. Due to the continuing problems with my below knee leg, I still used the PPAM-Aid, a blue balloon structure. The cushion is supposed to protect the damage done by the pressure of standing and moving into the legs, but it's always painful.

At first it was agony. The prosthesis is suction-pressurised around the knee and consists of a metal rod and a flexi foot. In wearing this all the weight is on the patella (kneecap). I have a right knee but no left, so with both prostheses fitted, and previously blessed with very long thigh bones, my left knee is longer than my right.

The sense of bodily invasion was overwhelming. If you've ever had a crown fitted to a tooth, or a dental brace, multiply that feeling of alien invasion a thousand-fold. On top of this was the sheer undisguised ugliness of it. I had to wear shorts at first so that the walking school physios could gauge my strides.

All the time, still, my brain was fighting for it simply not to be the case. This wasn't me. This wasn't who I was. I hated the feeling of being enclosed, imprisoned by plastics and silicones.

It was a case of mind over matter to get myself forward to the parallel bars to begin the next important stage of my journey. I still focussed specifically on Andrew's motorbike. If I could walk to his bike and sit on the pillion everything would be as it was and we would roar off away from this hell hole and into the sunset together.

Gradually I built up to walking up and down, up and down between the bars. Music was a great help. Working to the rhythm. Though I couldn't listen to many of my old favourite artists, they made me too sad, Peter

Gabriel's *Don't Give Up* got through. I'd play it at full volume on my Walkman as I marched up and down, over and over again.

Working the legs was painful. I had to wear woollen socks on each of the legs for cushioning, sometimes two when it got too painful. The left fitting was problematical at first, but generally the skin grafting healed well. Eventually I was able to manage with it, but the right leg will always be more of a problem due to my right "weak" knee. The hospital wanted to carry out further surgery to amputate more of my left thigh to balance the knees but I couldn't tolerate any more. It would have been for cosmetic reasons and wasn't necessary. I had lost enough.

The amount of concentration, sweat and stamina needed was immense. I had to learn to use a whole new set of muscle groups, going against everything nature had taught my body. I had to concentrate on a movement that was simply unnatural.

However, I made good progress. The joy of being able to walk was so overwhelming that I'd frequently overdo it. All the silicone and aluminium rubbing up against my skin caused soreness and chafing problems.

Moving away from the bars was a big step, literally. Even with two sticks to keep me steady, I needed the security of somebody there to catch me in case I fell. Everything within my vision – carpet, doorway, chair – became an obstacle.

I likened my task to a physical version of anorexics having to learn to eat again. When we learn as toddlers how to put one foot in front of the other whilst keeping our balance, the memory of the process becomes almost instantly sealed into the forgotten past. So at the age of 29 pushing on 30, my main task in life was to relearn a skill I hadn't been aware I'd ever had to master in the first place.

"Embodied Intelligence" is a subject at the forefront of Artificial Intelligence research. Psychologists and computer experts are still unravelling the mysteries, but what they are discovering, and what I very much came to realise at the time, is that it's your body as much as your mind that teaches you to walk. As with animals, the learning process is all bound up with instinct.

Poles of metal now walked for me and with me – a pair of iron stilts, without the prosthetic covers. With the parallel bars on each side of me, I worked hard on training the remaining muscles in my legs and the extra muscles in my back, very different muscles, to just keep putting one foot in front of the other, over and over and over again. I was fixing the walking procedure in my body, programming my mind to eventually follow along.

It took quite a time. Every tiny movement required thought. Perhaps the more rudimentary the body function is, the more complicated the thought process that accompanies it is, until it clicks back to automatic as the body takes over from the brain? I always believed in muscle memory, in the way that the body so cleverly remembers how to dance and how to ride a horse. And I soon learnt to be grateful that at least I had one knee, albeit a weak knee. The difference between my below knee and above knee leg – physically and prosthetically – is miles apart.

I made good progress. A few more compliments from the physioterrorists and my confidence levels overstretched themselves. I left the parallel bars behind and walked into the coffee shop area. I felt a slight dizziness as my legs and brain adjusted to the carpeted floor. I raised my head and panic hit me. It was too far to get to the other side of the room, my balance went and within a second I was arse over tit onto the brown industrial carpet, marooned on the Walking School floor, metal legs akimbo.

Physios raced to me, murmuring 'Are you OK?' and lifted me onto a chair.

Learning to cope with the "feel" of different floor surfaces was moving into an advanced level I wasn't ready for yet, though these days the phantom phenomenon does help me to walk. I feel the soles of my feet comfortably buzzing away. Because I have to be so aware of them at all times, I apparently feel my own legs far more than an able-bodied person. I don't have to look down to see them. Though, even today with years of practice, I do have to look down and pay more attention on unfamiliar terrain.

With most amputations, though phantoms are common at first, over time the feeling telescopes upwards until it becomes an aura of neuroactivity around the stump. This hasn't happened with me. Because the first major operation I had was a life-saving one, the surgeons had to slice through my nerves rather than take the more delicate route.

I can very much sense this cell-based energy still lurking. They aren't called phantom pain for nothing, They can literally take on a life of their own in sometimes bizarre, often painful, ways. In severe cold weather I sometimes get attacks where my legs and feet start juddering with spasms. The contractions accelerate and so does the pain. It's a bit like the worst toothache you can imagine. But because the pains are in the phantom parts and not "real" parts of my body, there's no painkiller that can treat them.

At the bizarre end of the spectrum, I was on holiday once in a sunny Spanish island feeling light, happy and carefree. I stopped at the side of a road to cross only for my legs to continue walking off over the road without me.

One of the world's foremost experts on the subject is neuroscientist Vilayanur S. Ramachandran, who I have met with to discuss my own experiences. His path of enquiry revolves around the idea of mind mapping where, with severe trauma, the nerve tracking systems in the brain move over into one another.

I was cross-examined after my fall. What I had eaten for breakfast? 'Nothing, as usual,' came my humiliated reply. A lecture followed on the energy required for the new walking process. It was compounded later that day when Nurse Paul came bounding into the ward kitchen where I was attempting to stand at the fridge door. The top half of my body swung with the movement of the fridge door which I held onto for dear life.

'You must eat, eat, eat Di. You use 180 percent additional energies in walking with two false legs.' He grabbed a sausage and began to waltz around the cramped space in the kitchen.

Gradually, as my determination set in, I grew good and strong and, as long as the other half of my double-act was there, I found plenty to laugh about. Laughter was absolutely essential at these times when the great tragedies of our fates were eyeballing us straight in the face. 'Can't walk can ye?' 'That's your life fucked right there, love.'

When the going got tough, we had mutual consent to curse at each other like pirates.

'Oy, Robocop,' get yer effing skates on, I'm leaving youse well behind.' Brett's cheeky face broke into a smile as I awkwardly turned on my new legs, sweating into the two sticks that were taking all of my weight.

Our relationship had progressed to pet names. Because of the amount of metal gadgetry I was walking on I'd become Robocop and he was Spit the Gadget – some small metal toy I'd picked up from a TV advert.

'Oh yeah, Spit, think you can go faster do you?' I responded, attempting to knock him over with a swipe of a wooden stick as I leaned against a cool wall and sighed.

I stood back up into the false limbs and tick-tacked my way across the wooden floor of the school. Cathy The One Legged Witch often shouted cheers of encouragement, as did Dear Tom, a lovely man, who hobbled around trussed up like a chicken, with straps holding his new leg on.

Tom and Cathy were both victims of diabetes. One day I unwittingly led them into rebellion on my birthday. Overloaded with delicious birthday cake I'd sneaked them pieces. After chomping their way through three slices of cake each they, and the medical staff, suffered the consequences. Blood sugar levels had soared along with my popularity. Unfortunately, the NHS medical bill moved up a few notches as they had to take the drugs to counteract the effects of the cake.

Every step I took was pain. It still is now. But I was buoyed up by the sheer exhilaration of being alive. I was alive. I was going to live and I was going to move around the world on the back of Andrew's motorbike. That feeling of escaping death by a whisper changes you forever.

CHAPTER EIGHTEEN

Sweet Love

Over the weeks it took me to adjust to my new, exhausting, regime the dreaded statement loomed but nobody pressured me. It would have to be done soon. But not yet. Meantime Coopers were accumulating some impressive evidence which helped to raise my spirits.

They'd put pressure on British Rail to return my Walkman, held since the accident by Victoria Transport Police. The headset was missing – casually thrown away because it had been "badly damaged and covered in blood". But two important pieces of evidence remained. The battery compartment had no cover and was empty and the cassette tape, which was still inside, had only played about half way through. This evidence irrevocably contradicted BR's official report which stated that the only thing to be recovered from the scene of the accident was my Walkman – which was still playing. Thus inferring that this is why I hadn't heard the guard shout "stand away".

The music was the American R&B soul and jazz singer-songwriter Anita Baker. Thank God it wasn't Eurythmics, Police or any other of my UK chart-topper favourites that could have suddenly taunted me at any muzac or radio-listening moment forever more.

Steve and Christopher Johnson re-examined the photos of the track taken by Andrew and Jonny and returned to the station armed with a pair of binoculars. There, four months after my accident, they discovered the batteries and Walkman battery cover still on the track. So much for BR's "enquiries".

Unfortunately, because getting down onto the track to retrieve the evidence would have been enough for BR to slap a trespass charge onto Coopers, they couldn't keep their discovery to themselves until a court reveal. Instead they arranged a meeting at the station with the BR man in charge on the day, one Peter Saville, Area Movements Inspector, South Central Movements Inspector's Office, Victoria.

Mr Saville confirmed that he'd arrived twenty minutes after the accident and had taken the driver and guard's statements. He hadn't interviewed anyone else, he said, as the priority had been to get me to hospital and the transport system up and running again. He said they'd made enquiries for witnesses but nobody had come forward.

Steve Hampshire and Christopher Johnson also did some timings and measurements, marking the exact spot where I fell down and the exact spot where I'd ended up. Their re-enactment of my hurry down the steps contradicted the ticket collector's statement that the train was already moving when I'd run past him. The train would have picked up far too much speed by the time I'd reached the platform. They also, in their thoroughness, realised that the ticket collector couldn't actually see the platform from his booth.

They also put further questions to our witnesses. Maggie Davis said there may have been a Walkman but she certainly didn't see or hear one on or near me, either after the accident or when I'd pushed past her at the barrier on the footbridge.

Kate Lowe didn't notice one. Nor did John Lowe who was sure he would have registered if I'd been wearing headphones and related it to the accident.

Maggie didn't see the train pull out but heard it and confirmed that the train definitely hadn't started when I passed them. She didn't hear the guard shouting stand clear or blow a whistle before the train moved. Nor did John and Kate. Nor did Debbie, sitting in the 4th carriage, very close to the accident, with the window half open.

The healthier I became, the more difficult it was to cope. Steve began nagging me constantly for the statement but I simply didn't have the inner resources to get my memories of that awful day down on paper. Each drug was gradually eliminated from my routine, from morphinates to heroin, through to a mixed dose of aspirin and analgesic.

As the medical care dwindled so the social care was increased.

"Rehabilitation", grounded in practicality and form filling, became a daily part of my existence. Forms for new housing; the mortgage and bill payments from a home I would no longer live in; for legal aid on my case; disability allowances for the future; applications for a new driving licence and masses of paperwork for a company that, with Sarah, I was still trying to run from my hospital bedroom. My status in life had changed so irrevocably, I felt reduced to a governmental statistic, with the word "disabled" stamped across everything I encountered.

I couldn't relate to the word at all. I always felt that one disabled a computer, you can't disable a person, there is still something of them there, a spirit, a movement of sorts, a life that, in most cases, should be lived. I was deeply concerned about getting back to work with my new status. I thought very hard about who I had ever seen or met in Cannes who had some type of disability – there was one guy, a brilliant self-made businessman but he had no real "outward" signs of disability. I knew in advance that I didn't want to wear disability as a badge. As an excuse.

The love from my wonderful family and my close friends kept me on the stable side of sanity. And I still had Andrew. Though if I ever tried to bring up any aspect of my future, or our future together, he would change the subject and prevaricate, he was still my boyfriend. I didn't know what he was thinking and was too ill to push for an open discussion. I had no true concept then of what had happened to me, of how much my life was going to have to change. He tended to arrive with his mates in tow, in hindsight probably to prevent me from getting emotionally heavy with him. I had said the "L" word after all. Although he didn't know in what context I uttered it, he knew that my focus in those Walking School times was "to get back to normal" for him.

Aware of how my emotional state was dependent on him, Helen had taken Andrew to the pub a couple of times to try to crack open his stiff upper lip cover and discover how he was really feeling. The first time the only thought he could express was: 'Why didn't I see Di that night, then it would not have happened? Why didn't I arrange to meet her?'

The second time, after Helen had got a few beers down him to loosen his tongue, he reiterated, 'I just wish things were back to normal.'

Then came a surprise visit that challenged my Andrew fixation, if only for a couple of hours. I'd just finished playing a game of cards with nurse Alice one day and was wondering if I could be arsed to get myself into my wheelchair to go outside for a cigarette when in walked Max.

All six feet tall, striding in to my stinky disinfectanty green room, albeit heavily disguised with top note of the Clarins perfume that Dinah had brought me for the purpose. *Eau Dynaminsante*. To this day, its perfume takes me straight back to that room and that time.

'Ah so you knew I wasn't going anywhere,' I joked but inside I was totally quaking – horrified.

Sarah had told me he was flying over but I'd told her to tell him not to come. I didn't think I could face him. I didn't want him to see me like this. The irreversible situation I had to endure could only be made worse by meeting up again. I wanted him to remember me as I was when we'd made mad, passionate love. With Max I'd always felt so beautiful.

Part of me also thought that if he and I had been together, the accident wouldn't have happened because I would have been in New York. But within minutes sheer delight had taken over and we were chatting away as if we'd never parted.

I'd forgotten it was a special beauty inside he made me feel as well as on the surface. He brought out the best in me. As with Andrew, we laughed a lot; but Max also totally understood the importance of my work to me and recognised the quiet ambition still in me. I wanted to get back to working again and we talked about that. I felt simply exquisite in his company. There were awkward moments. Hugging was difficult for me – I couldn't stand to have anyone near my lower body, but we explored this reaction together. He was one of the few people that handled my clumsy awkwardness well and our discussion soon became as deep as they had been previously.

'Where do you think your legs are now?'

'They were probably put in a skip and then burnt.'

'But where are they Di?'

'They are still with me, Max. They are telling me that they didn't want to go.'

For a few precious hours my troubles came secondary to the precious moments we were sharing and I felt as beautiful as I'd ever been in my life again.

As a senior executive, Max had a car and driver at his disposal wherever he went. It shows what a good person he is that in coming to see me he decided to take the overland train so that he could try to understand what I'd been through. In doing that his wedding ring caught on the door-handle, twisting it.

I had no illusions. No illusions at all, but I appreciated so much his effort to come and see me. His parting words were, 'See you in Cannes in April.'

I didn't tell Andrew about Max's visit. There was no point. In my thinking of the time, it was vital that I didn't upset him any more than I had done so already by having my accident, and Max was squarely in my past now. Just as my relationship with Duncan had developed into a real friendship. Chef Dunky had become an amazing friend, often cooking and delivering the most incredible dishes into the hospital.

I had no idea at the time that he was still hoping we'd get back together.

CHAPTER NINETEEN

Desperado

My days were filled with a tough routine of gym work, physiotherapy (me throwing bean bags at a physioterrorist) and severe walking training interjected with endless smatterings of paperwork.

As far as walking was concerned, I'd become a woman possessed. Marching up and down the bars when everyone else was resting or eating – the image of me on the back of Andrew's motorbike fixed in my mind.

I was becoming a little more used to leaving the hospital, with all the preparations that it involved, and was being allowed out more. The wedding had been hard to bear and I still had feelings of shame and embarrassment to overcome but I was determined that my thirtieth birthday would be a more positive experience. For the first time I was given leave to stay at Andrew's for the whole weekend.

Sarah had bought me a new outfit, a chiffon ballerina skirt and a floaty cream jacket.

Andrew had disappointed me again, bringing me a brown paper wrapping of a present. Inside was a toiletry bag. I'd laughed it off with genuine humour because lovely Annie Keaveney had just previously brought in a beautiful present and a special signed photo from Sting, whose music I loved. I took extra care with my make-up, thinking tonight, perhaps, I'll show Andrew what he's been missing all these weeks.

Twenty-five friends gathered around a long table at a local wine bar/restaurant. As they sang Happy Birthday I looked around at all of them thinking well, at least I made it to thirty.

When the evening ended we had the difficult process of getting the wheelchair into Susan and John's tiny car and all of us squeezing in. I was so excited to be staying away from hospital for the weekend, tweaking

Andrew's thigh as he drove us back to his flat. I was nervous and hadn't been able to have a drink due to the medication I was still taking.

It was very disturbing to return to a place I'd previously skipped in and out of. I viewed everything with more clarity, the colours of doors as he shoved me through them, the height and width of everything. I scanned the lounge where we'd first begun our love-making. It was alien, I couldn't relate to the size of it. From the wheelchair I saw everything as a child. It was a shock. Andrew held me as best he could. It involved crouching and leaning his body to get hold of me in the chair. He kissed me and I could hear by his breathing that he was becoming aroused.

I pushed my way into the bedroom and quickly got out of the wheelchair, undressed into a nightie from my overnight bag and sat up in bed as he came back from the loo. Our kissing led to lovemaking. Andrew trembled, worried, I think, about hurting me. My legs were covered in bandages and I tried to keep them hidden under the bedclothes. It was over in minutes and I felt utter relief that I'd done it, rather than any post-coital passion. Andrew fell asleep and I had a cigarette, looking at his peaceful face lit by the street lamps through the thin curtains.

I woke early to see Andrew getting dressed.

'I'm going to the gym with Susan and John.'

He'd never been to the gym before. What happened the night before dissolved from my mind. He was trying to pull away from me. I couldn't possibly go to the gym. I couldn't even walk for Christ's sake.

I dressed, ate a piece of dry toast and switched on the television. I hardly noticed the screen in Roehampton, it was there as background wallpaper. But now my mind became alert to all the adverts. And legs. Beautiful long, slim healthy legs. Models with exquisite faces and bodies staring at me, mouthing promises of chocolate bars and silky tights. I was frozen on the bed, looking at the flickering screen of images, believing that I would never be sexually attractive ever again. Legs seemed so important to the complete sexual image and I wept at my loss, grieving for my limbs as if they were people. They had been my friends and now they were gone.

Andrew returned looking hot and sweaty. I tried to keep up a light conversation but he was distracted. Finally he plucked up his words and stuttered them out.

'I was thinking I'd take you back tonight.'

My heart stopped. 'Tonight?' I gasped. 'To hospital? But I'm allowed a whole weekend. It's a very special arrangement, with the consultant's permission.'

'I'm sorry Di, but I've arranged to go Motocrossing tomorrow, and it's an early start.'

I was defenceless against such a decision. Totally dependent, I sobbed quietly all the way back to the dreary ward, a silent and miserable place at weekends. I had no visitors because everyone believed I was off having a wonderful time with my beau.

'Bastard,' I called to the air. 'Rotten stinking life.' I raised my fist, and punched at whoever was up there.

And then I prayed. A fervent prayer. 'I will win him back. I will walk. I will battle on and win him back.'

Andrew came in late that night. He'd fallen asleep on the train, his bike having broken down. I saw these as fateful signs that were trying to tell me something. He was affectionate but I was gradually coming to recognise a look of burned grief in his eyes and a distance in his voice. I tried to remain optimistic.

'I'll be walking soon!'

'That's great, Di! Perhaps you'll be up and about by the time I get back from my holiday.'

I felt a jerk of tension in my stomach. 'What holiday?'

'Mum and Dad are taking me to Prague.'

'When!'

'About two weeks' time.'

'That's lovely!' I said, thinking 'bastards'.

'I'll be back in the middle of November.'

'November? They're taking you away for three weeks?'

'Great isn't it!' he smiled his false smile, a smile that indicated friendliness and nothing more.

I couldn't say anything. My mood had plummeted. As he whistled his way off down the corridor, I lay listening to his feet clumping slowly away.

CHAPTER TWENTY

Somewhere

A week before his departure, Andrew took me out for an Indian meal.

We munched and crunched our way through poppadoms and curry and spoke about the future. He seemed slightly ambiguous but any glint of hopeful thought on his part was snaffled up by my imagination and exaggerated to a form of commitment. The clearest picture from the evening however, was the opinion that if Andrew didn't talk to someone, he was likely to become introverted and in need of therapy.

Over pudding I attempted to prise some emotion, any emotional feelings he had with regard to the accident. All he could muster was a comment on the amount of blood there had been on that terrible day of the accident.

'They were running out of bandages, Di, they were dashing around for dressings, they could not stop the bleeding, there was blood everywhere.'

Not only was I shocked that he'd witnessed this scene, I was stunned that it was me he was talking about. I remembered telling him that I loved him, wanted to say now that I thought these would be my last words – ever. And the love I declared was for everyone I knew, who would miss me. I hadn't registered that he was clearly in some form of post- traumatic shock himself. What I feared was that his parents were to be the altars of truth on which Andrew would lay all his grief. No problem for him – but I knew that there would be heavy persuasion on the issue of living his life with someone as injured as I.

'Jane in tonight?' I asked Brett the morning after Andrew had gone.

Jane was Brett's sweet devoted girlfriend. I envied their relationship, so sure in their affection for each other, even though a tornado had reshaped their lives the night Brett had piled into a traffic bollard on his motorbike.

'Yeah she'll be in. What about Andrew?'

I shook my head and sighed again.

'Naah, he's gone off to Prague for a holiday,' I said casually. 'We said our goodbyes last night.'

The goodbyes had consisted of Andrew standing outside my hospital room in the cold autumnal air, passing a cigarette through the window. We'd watched one third of a video – *The Lady and The Tramp*. As the doggies in the cartoon started kissing through the spaghetti Andrew stood up abruptly from the bed and declared it was time to go. A frown of guilt crossed his forehead as he gave me a cursory kiss on the mouth. We'd earlier been fumbling under the bedclothes but were disturbed by a nurse. He walked outside, lit up his cigarette and half stuck his head through the window.

Determined not to cry, I watched him make his way across the hospital car park.

'I'll be walking next time you see me,' I called as my inner voice screamed, 'Don't go. Don't go.'

I sat silently in my wheelchair at the window watching his bike tear off into the night. To freedom.

I talked about my doubts over Andrew with close girlfriends who agreed with me that he should be left to his own devices. That I should never call him and, returning to my original theory, that he should only visit when he felt like it. Though I felt more desperate than ever, I mustn't let him know that.

'There's more than one way to skin a sausage,' my friend Dinah would say. I recognised that there was no point being with someone who didn't want to be with me, but it was too late. My heart had begun to rule my head. I couldn't comprehend meeting anyone else in my new situation. I had to win Andrew over.

My determination mixed with sadness soon turned to determination peppered with anger. A concentrated power I used at Walking School over the following weeks.

It was all about balance. Without the proper false legs, all I could practise was standing upright and walking in the bars. I wore a Sony Walkman and walked and walked the bars until the ends of my legs bled.

Steve Hampshire called to fill me in on exactly what they wanted in my statement. It was upsetting to discover that I had to include information about my status before the accident as well as the event itself, and all in as much detail as I could muster, but it couldn't be put off any longer. I set aside a quiet afternoon, put all visitors on hold and locked myself into the tortuous past, gulping with pain and fear as I typed.

Paul came in after I'd finished and asked if he could read it.

I studied his face as he read through my words. He looked sad but at the end he put it on the bed and said quietly, 'Um, it reads like a bad novel doesn't it Di?'

This comment spawned the *Mills and Boon* Lurve campaign. From that moment one nurse in particular, Hannilay, a superficially frosty Swedish lady, was "Love-Bombed". Her ward round would continually be interrupted as Paul and I, "The Lurve Team", would follow her as she administered to various patients, giving a running commentary on their care.

'Lovingly Hannilay caressed the patient's taut thigh. Her velvety touch sent him into paroxysms of desire. Slowly she unbuttoned the front of her uniform.'

'Enough,' Hannilay would call, suppressing laughter, determined to get on with her work.

But still Paul and I would hover at the door.

'Hannilay's eyes blazed with fury,' Paul went on. 'She reached for the cool smooth enema tube, her hands shaking with anticipation...'

And I would continue, '...her uniform swung open to reveal black patent thigh length boots. They rustled and creaked as slowly she moved towards the man...'

My day of discharge into the outside world was drawing closer. I was going to miss Paul, and Brett, terribly.

CHAPTER TWENTY-ONE

Feel It In My Bones – Paul Usher

The hospital social worker became a daily visitor to my room. With kindness and patience, Carol helped me face up to the practicalities by leading me through the maze of forms. We decided that I should try and find somewhere to live close to work – in Wandsworth.

Is there anyone you know with ground floor living space Diana?' she asked. 'In case there is a delay in finding you something?'

I surprised myself with the bitter tears that rose in my throat.

'Andrew.'

'Oh!'

'Ironically, Carol, he's the only person in this country, of all my five hundred and fifty visitors, who has a bedroom and bathroom on the ground floor.'

She held my gaze and asked the next question without speaking.

'But no,' I muttered. 'This is all about dependency. I will not be dependent on him. He would have to make the offer.'

My friends in the television industry were more forthcoming. To help me adjust to my new life, they'd set up a benefit trust. The aim was to raise a bit of cash to enable me to move home without too much strain.

Launched at MIPCOM, the TV market in Cannes in October, money was already beginning to arrive. I was flattered, relieved and thankful for people's kindness. I was also in a state of shock that I was now having to turn to an industry for help. Also slightly humiliated that some of my friends were literally asking for money from people who'd previously been my peer group. Instead of dealing with them on a business level I was now a charity. Though delighted at the thought of some much-needed funding, I was inwardly uncomfortable with the idea of people donating money to someone they could be doing business with again in the near future.

However, it raised my spirit and was something I could focus on that was positive.

Andrew sent me a postcard from Prague. He mentioned the amazing price of beer (seven pence a pint) and how beautiful the city was. He signed it "love" which I briefly and sentimentally tried to read much into, but nothing more was revealed in his hasty handwriting. I slept with it under my pillow and, despite a fun evening with a couple of friends that day, endured a night of staring at the ceiling, silent tears rolling down my face, grinding my teeth at the prospect of a bleak future.

The love and attention of my family and friends kept me alive through those awful doubting moments with Andrew. A few days later, another unexpected visitor arrived.

I woke to exhaustion and a grey November morning, the ward quiet and cold. A short tap at my door preceded Jackie, the ward sister coming in with a bright smile on her face and an aura of flirtation.

'A visitor Diana and so early! We recognise him off the telly but I think he thinks he's in disguise!' She paused, before adding with a low voice, 'He's rather dishy isn't he?'

'Two minutes Jackie, and then send him in.' Feeling like a character from a Jane Austen novel welcoming characters into a parlour, I lunged for my toothbrush and make-up bag and combed my fingers through my hair.

There was a loud knock on the door.

'Ushy!' I squealed.

Paul Usher, or Barry Grant from *Brookside,* was one of the most popular soap actors in the country at the time. I'd met him on my first day as a PR girl on the show and we developed a close friendship rooted in our life loves of humour and music.

"Have you f***ed Barry Grant?" was the question asked of me constantly by his obsessed fans who stalked him absolutely everywhere. If they couldn't get close to him they'd take me as the next best. One time I had to sign autographs on a train from London to Liverpool – two and a half hours of writing, "I know Barry Grant, Love Diana Hill".

We hugged and kissed and hugged again. He placed two bananas and some roses on the bed.

'The flowers are from me the bananas are from Jim-Jam.' Jim-Jam, or James, was Paul's son. He gently pushed the wheelchair at the side of my bed out of the way and half lay next to me, his arm under my head.

We reminisced over anecdotes from the years at Brookside and beyond.

'It was the best of times, the worst of times,' I giggled with Paul as we lay on the bed. Our friendship had remained just that – despite some close calls to the nature of sexual attraction. I was glad of it then as I could snuggle up to him and talk on a deep level about what had happened to me.

We talked about the drugs I was gradually being weaned from. He was especially interested in the euphoria brought on by the morphinated drugs.

'You enjoy your beach holidays,' I said. 'Imagine then that you have been on holiday for a long stretch, with all cares in the world greatly diminished. Your body is very relaxed, your mind likewise. Your body is severely damaged but you feel extremely healthy, content and happy. I would estimate one dose of morphine is equal to about one week in the sun and sea. They also help you to accept what's happened to you. One reason no doubt why they give morphine to patients dying of cancer.'

'Did you get addicted?'

'Only in the physical sense – more pain creeping through as they lowered the doses but those doses are very cleverly managed. I noticed this especially as I came off the tablet form of heroin, which only ever killed pain. The amount was so adeptly calculated it produced no euphoria whatsoever. Sometimes on the drugs rounds they'd miss my room out, and sometimes they missed me out altogether. I never asked for them unless I was in agony. I don't wish to be on them now. I want absolute reality in my life now, Ushy. I want to feel happiness again without the crutch, the support that drugs can offer.'

We talked on for a couple of hours. With Paul, and with many other close friends, I'd not experienced the opportunities to talk quite so deeply about life before. These attempts to seek out my inner core of spirituality and strength combined with the solace of friendship were helping to create a well of strength that I didn't know I had. The emotional sensation was 'This cannot get any worse, and even if it does, I shall make it better. I shall work through this until it gets better.'

He left with the words, 'It'll be a battle Di, but you'll do it.'

I felt a well of emptiness rise up in me as he left, but held it in check, clasping the crystal cross round my neck. This had become my "white light" in the dark times when I dug and prayed continually for more and more strength.

That quiet Saturday afternoon I gradually felt recharged. With most patients away for the weekend, I donned the iron legs and walked up and down the parallel bars, listening to upbeat music through headphones.

CHAPTER TWENTY-TWO

Pretty Woman

My discharge back into the outside world was getting closer, with no more idea of where I would be living. For a while I considered moving to a different part of London, as far as possible from the scene of the accident. The reality was the opposite. I really had to find somewhere closer, rather than further away from, the scene if I was planning to continue working at my company. I also would need to be within easy reach of the hospital for future regular appointments, which continue to this day.

Despite Andrew not offering to have me stay, even for a short while as I adapted to the outside world, my determination to keep him hadn't altered.

Duncan continued to visit regularly, bringing delicious treats he'd made for me. After a heart to heart discussion one day he finally realised that we were never going to be. He started dating again and I was pleased. We'd survived into true friendship with our relationship cemented into the past.

The intensive walking training had given me some confidence. I was walking around the wards now and had even attempted to walk down a kerb. The slight process (completed with no thought whatsoever in the past) of stepping in downward motion had produced tears and the words, "I just can't do it". But, bolstered by kind but firm physios, and one in particular, a personable chap called David, I kept trying until the fear had abated. I began to learn that the only way to keep the intense fear under control was to actually "walk" through it. To do what I feared so much.

My next hurdle was to face the real world – with the legs on.

David joined me on my first trip out of hospital without the wheelchair. It was fitting that it was a business trip. Work was my main thrust for getting back into the stream of daily living and out of the claustrophobic walls of my hospital room.

Sarah came to pick us up. Our destination was Pinewood Film Studios, a half an hour or so drive out of London. Assisted by David, with Sarah rushing ahead to hold the heavy swinging doors, I hobbled my way into the poky photography room where the source of work lay. I was to choose the publicity photos to accompany the international sale of a Barbara Taylor Bradford mini-series starring Lindsay Wagner. Before the accident and in good light this would have taken me seconds. I took my time, humming and ha'ing over the glossy photos. Eventually the old skills of perception, of what makes a picture great instead of good, came back to me and I began to enjoy myself. Then the Pinewood publicity guy joined us. His calm exterior revealed itself to be a lie. He was a typically hysterical press merchant, put on this earth to creep to studio heads and patronise anyone else.

'No no no,' he began, as he frantically picked up my photo choices. 'Her hair looks *awful* on that one.'

'It looks immaculate to me,' I fired back, holding my ground.

'It's the wrong colour. Oh Jesus, it's the wrong colour.' He slapped his hand to his head like a war-torn widow. 'She had to have it re-coloured half way through the shoot. It was peachy, golden blonde. We can't have this photo.'

I looked at him and stared. His hand was still over one eye, as if in physical pain.

My trousers had ridden up, revealing two iron poles of ankle. I hated him at that moment and I hated what he represented. Fussing about the shade of someone's hair. It was an incident that I would have bitten my lip over in the past. A tale to laugh about later, but not now. I just stared at him, my heart pounding in anger and disgust. Sarah looked at me with scared eyes. I recovered my professionalism just in time, smiled and conceded to his hair-do hysteria. But I wanted to scream at him.

David helped me out of the seat and into the car.

'And I was worried about getting back to the real world,' I hissed at him as I hoisted myself into the passenger seat.

We drove back in silence. I stared down grumpily at the two unnatural legs in front of me, comparing them with Sarah's as she smoothly operated the car. I was losing my sense of wonder at having survived. That ever contentious issue. The way a person looks, was beginning to erode into my very sense of being.

Andrew was due back from his holiday and I tried to calm the mounting nerves. Would his parents' little scheme, in the form of three weeks' break away from me, have worked? I spent a painful morning on the legs in the physio's tiny kitchen, attempting to regain my culinary skills. I produced an overdone spaghetti for Brett, who hovered at the door like a salivating wolf. I wished so much that it had been Andrew who'd been shovelling his way through my recipe dish. Would I ever cook for Andrew again?

On the day before his return, I also learnt to get on a motorbike. This was to be my big surprise for him. The boyfriend of one of the physios brought in his monster machine and, after much heavy breathing and maneuvering I finally sat astride. I was so proud of my achievement, knowing that Andrew couldn't fail but to be impressed.

The day didn't get off to a good start. Todd, the prosthetist, had needed my false legs back to make complicated final technical adjustments and to prepare the synthetic flesh covers that would hide the metal and fibreglass elements. The timing couldn't be worse and I pleaded for their return before the evening. I was distraught without my body armour. Although extremely painful they had provided me with a semblance of wholeness. Most of the time I'd only been able to sit in a wheelchair with them on, but they'd added an extra dimension to my being. They suggested a whole body. The promise of walking. Instead I sat in my wheelchair waiting for Andrew to arrive with the catastrophic feeling of sitting there with no legs. A mermaid with no siren powers, stranded on dry land.

We were going out to a restaurant. I'd gone to town on the hair, make-up and outfit, disguising my lack of prosthetics with the swathes of material provided by a long, floaty skirt.

'Fuck me Di, you scrub up well,' commented a passing Brett.

I hurled a few fruity words at him. With one of those universal "bloke not understanding the ways of women" shrugs, he turned and ran — as much as he could on his new prosthetic.

The nurses too were full of compliments, but I didn't believe any of them. The wheelchair felt like a rock beneath me.

Andrew arrived without fanfare, funny, emotional or otherwise, gave me a quick peck on the cheek, heaved the wheelchair around and began pushing me towards the door.

'Oh!' he suddenly stopped and felt in his pockets. 'I nearly forgot…'

Wondering for a moment if the coolness had been a charade of some kind, my heart lifted. I smiled as he passed me a box.

I opened it. Inside was a hand-carved wooden cigarette box.

'I've given up,' he said quietly. 'But I thought you would like that.'

The tone for the evening was set.

The restaurant was an up-market burger place with straws for every drink and a popcorn machine that popped and cracked its way into our conversations.

I told Andrew of my walking school adventures, omitting all the pain and despair and highlighting the humour and tit-bits of fun. He listened in a distracted way, toyed with his food and spoke superficially of Prague. He'd spent most of his time in the student haunts, seeking out non-emotional, philosophically-driven conversations with total strangers.

'Oh, and guess what?' I had saved my big news for dessert. 'I got on a motorbike!'

I waited for his reaction. It was a long time coming.

'Oh that's good.' He forked some burger. 'This is quite good nosh you know,' he said. And then, as if it couldn't get any worse, added, 'Do you remember when we burnt all the meat on the barbeque?'

'That wasn't me. You've told me that story before. It was with Janine.'

He winced at the sound of her name. If I'd slapped him it would have had the same effect. He was confusing me with the fiancé who'd dumped him. I realised that he was suffering the pain her desertion had brought and wasn't even thinking about my dilemma. It was as if he'd moved back in grief and couldn't bear to contemplate dwelling on what I, or we as a supposed couple, were having to face. I swung the conversation around to us, straining for just a particle of feeling on his current situation.

'We weren't together a long time,' he spoke in the past tense. 'We didn't know each other very well before all this,' he nodded in the direction of under the table, where my stunted legs lay hanging. 'Did we Di?'

Did we? It was like a plea. Tears circled my eyes. I looked at him, unblinking, refusing to let the waiting tears drop onto my cheeks.

'I'm feeling a bit burdened. It was good to get away.' He smiled but his eyes also glistened slightly.

He wants to finish it, here in this restaurant, a public place, I thought. I wanted to get hysterical and throw a few plates around but I had to remain calm, I was going to need the restaurant staff to get back to the hospital. He's a bloody coward.

Did my face register such panic and dismay? For he suddenly hinted at the future with a "let's get back to normal shall we?" comment. My ribcage thudded with relief. He left for the loo and I wiped away rogue tears. I remained outwardly steady but my soul whispered to me that it was just a matter of time now. "Back to normal?" my mind rattled the question around. How is that ever going to be possible?

'Fuck him,' said Brett back at the hospital. I didn't tell him what had happened but he sensed something right away. He was paralytically drunk, and legless.

'Fuck'em all, we're partying tonight, my beautiful Di and don't you even think of not turning up.'

It was a leaving party. Brett's new leg was ready and he'd be going home the following day. I knew it was coming but it was another bombshell. 'Let's get back to normal shall we?' I replayed Andrew's words over and over in my mind as I wheeled my way up the long, dark corridor towards the crack of light that slanted from Brett's room, and the sound of The Eagles' *Desperado* played its mournful tune.

"We"? We were still "we". There was hope there and I had to hold onto it.

The music seemed a fitting tribute to my soul's deliberations. How I'd longed to be in my legs, to stand up from the wheelchair, to put my arms around Andrew and to have given him a long and passionate kiss. Instead of which I'd become so quiet in the restaurant that even he'd had to ask 'Anything wrong?'

My heart bleeding tears, I'd shaken my head.

Brett had lined up empty cans around his room and had now progressed to "spirit mode".

'Come on Di, ave one of these.'

I sipped at the rim of the plastic cup and then bit it, feeling sick with grief. It was a mixture of vodka, Bacardi and coke.

'Paddy nicked a bottle of pure morphine,' said Brett. 'He only tried to get into bed with Cathy the Witch. She was going to accept,' he hiccuped. Breathing deeply, he went on. 'But Jackie caught them at it, hee hee hee.'

Despite myself I smiled. And then laughed. We looked into each others' eyes. Dear Brett, going home to his caring adoring girlfriend who'd look after him. I would miss him deeply.

'You'll be sorted soon,' he said gently. If it wasn't for my housing problem I would have been going home as well. 'Part of me doesn't want to leave here you know, Di. Can you believe that, after all this shit? I really love you Di. You're like a sister to me.'

I smiled again, pleased at the compliment but wondering if I'd now be a sister to every man I had known or would ever meet.

A few days later Todd Drew called me down to the workshop where the technicians were working on my legs. Unlike the brave, macho male amputees, the army lads, the motor bikers, who wore their prosthetics naked, all metal exposed, who wore their physical losses as a badge of honour, I was a woman and feminine disguise was the key. Mine lay there on a small table, mannequined limbs ready to be finally shaped to the look I requested. I sat in my wheelchair, calling over the noise of the technician's noisy electric tools.

'Go on, more off the ankles.'

'We've shaved as much as we can, we're nearly down to the metal.'

'Oh please, Just a smidgen, think Betty Grable. Insured for a million.'

The song *Pretty Woman* by Roy Orbison began to play out of the tinny radio standing amongst the tools.

'Think Julia Roberts,' I yelled. 'Does she have fat ankles? No she does not. Go on, just a little bit more.'

As the technician whistled and ground away at the foam covering I sat and listened to the song about a pretty woman walking down a street.

The words scratched at my feelings. I felt very tired and craved the type of long sleep where you wake up and feel much better.

Andrew had phoned but only to cancel coming in at lunchtime. He'd been in only once, briefly, since our evening out, but his eyes had flashed wild distraction. He was only interested in the purely consequential. Minor anecdotes like how attractive my girlfriends were. What I'd eaten. He was, I noticed, putting on substantial amounts of weight. I dug deeply into my heart and soul for strength, for the power and guidance not to care what he did, but it was not forthcoming. In the canteen that morning, I'd told Helen of our evening out and to my dismay she didn't offer the usual 'Don't worry, it'll be alright,' scenario. Her eyes had clouded over briefly and she replied with one word, 'Shit'. She knew a substantial part of my emotional recovery lay at Andrew's door and that door seemed to be closing.

The moment the legs were finally finished I raced my wheelie down to the Walking School to try them on. I felt sick to the stomach when I saw the piggy-pink looking revolting things. Swallowing hard, I patiently put them on as I'd been taught. I sat down, stood up and turned around in them, looking down at the thick, pink foam strapped so uncomfortably where my slender legs had once been. The colour could easily be changed with the use of stockings, they said over and over, trying to soothe me. Ignoring the pain that ripped into my own legs, and the leather belt that gripped my waist like a vice to hold the above-knee leg on, I took a couple of faltering steps. It was even tougher with the coverings on the false legs – they'd made them very stiff.

I had no choice but to persevere. By the end of the morning I'd successfully walked the length of the Walking School.

I so wished Brett had been there.

CHAPTER TWENTY-THREE

Chains

During this lonely, uncertain phase of my recuperation, support continued to reach through to me from the world outside, keeping my faith in the immense kindness of friends and strangers high.

This letter arrived one day, addressed to my surgeon, from a man who'd been on duty at the local electricity sub station that evening.

Sometimes when I go to bed I lie awake thinking of her. I see her tripping down those stairs happy and carefree on that lovely warm late summer evening – and all of her life in front of her. Then disaster strikes. I have no words for it. I would very much like to hear from you at your convenience to hear how the lady is getting on. Give her my very kind regards and tell her that she is always in my thoughts. Sincerely, Robert A Perkins. PS I apologise for writing on a piece of my work paper.

Knowing there are such people in the world, strangers who can feel so deeply for people they've never met, was a revelation.

Shortly afterwards over £3,000 (around $4,450) suddenly appeared in my bank account – the money raised by my friends and colleagues at MIPCOM in Cannes. Stunned by this discovery, Sarah and I agreed that a little retail therapy might be in order. We decided to take my new legs out for a little "girly" shopping trip.

I'd noticed pre-accident that Kingston, south-west London's largest shopping region, seemed to be well set up for wheelchair access. This was unusual. In the post-war town planning systems of the 1950s and 60s, disabled access wasn't an afterthought, it simply hadn't existed. In the late 1980s Kingston had become one of the first towns in the UK to adopt the US-style Shopping Mall experience.

This was a novelty and a godsend, disabled access wouldn't become the norm like this for another decade at least. I circled and wheeled my way around the clothes department of Bentalls with ease. I tried to hold my head up, ignoring the stares that focussed my way. The looks said, "what's wrong with her?" or "poor thing, she's different so we'll have a good look". I suppose disabled people weren't so visible then in the general community, but I couldn't fathom how people could stare at me with such concentration when they must have known how embarrassing it was for anybody to be openly gawked at.

I grabbed a load of appealing jackets and trousers in Jaeger and headed for the dressing room. Sweat poured from my forehead as I huffed and puffed my way into the clothing and stood, legs shaking, and looked at myself in the long mirrors. It was me, but it didn't look like me. The beautiful jacket looked good but the false above-knee leg stuck out dramatically to the side of the trousers, as if I had stuffed an ironing board in it with my legs. I tried to stand without the sticks, sideways on, ignoring the leg that stuck out. I had never, in the past, considered spending so much money on clothes. Now that I could, I was determined to look reasonable. Which I did if I stood in one position, completely still, much like a top fashion model in an awkward pose. It required me to lean against the partition wall to achieve this effect and of course the partition wall, being temporary, leaned with me and fell down. Half of the store's personnel seemed to appear from nowhere. All grabbing at me to get me up.

'Just pass me a chair, please,' I groaned, unhurt but deeply humiliated.

I bought everything and was subjected to further distress on payment. The shop assistant had seen me pick the clothes from the rails, she had popped her nosey head around the curtains to see "How I was getting on", in trying them on. She'd not tried to help me get up and yet, when it came to paying she turned to Sarah for payment. I sat and looked at her, from the wheelchair, unable to speak at the insult.

'Oh sorry dear, I thought your friend would be, er, paying,' was her response as I held out my gold credit card. Another stereotype box ticked for those with disabilities – Are you disabled – tick. Are you therefore poor/undervalued/of no economic value – tick.

Undeterred, in fact, wheeling around now to the strain of inner anger, we headed for the shoe department. I chose three pairs of shoes, all size seven, knowing that I could squeeze them onto the false feet whether they fitted or not. They just had to have the correct heel size for walking purposes.

'Would madam like me to help put them on?' said the young man as he brought out the boxes.

'No just wrap them without the packaging please,' I replied.

'But madam, some of the sized may differ very slightly. For comfort, I really think that you should.'

'You see these,' I interrupted, raising my feet from the wheelchair footplate. 'They're false. I don't think Madam needs to try them on, do you dear?'

He blushed purple. I enjoyed a quiet little smirk with Sarah as he raced to the till.

I flashed that gold card for the next two hours, only stopping for financial breath as we sipped coffee and delved into the large glossy carrier bags that swung from the wheelchair handles.

Back on the ward Sarah and a few other friends who were visiting hung the clothes around the room, covering the walls with beautiful colours and folds of materials. I lay on the bed, exhausted, and looked at them. They meant nothing.

If I'd been able, I would have thrown every one of those items of clothing around my room, Gatsby–style.

Breaking my "not asking Andrew for anything" rule for once, I'd phoned him to see if he wanted to come and see my spoils. He'd declined. I felt sick with fear and could literally feel the walls of claustrophobic depression moving in on me. I couldn't stop thinking of Brett and his girlfriend at home. I asked my other friends to leave early and sat in my wheelchair by the window, looking out onto a dark rain-streaked world, swallowing despair and praying for strength.

The deep unhappiness I was trying to control in order to display a reasonable attitude to the outside world was depleting my energy reserves rapidly. Christmas, the time of dread for those suffering under the mantle of grief, trauma and any recent bereavement, was looming. I knew I had to act quickly to restore a sense of purpose to my life. I debated with myself the best course of action.

Then took it.

After phoning Duncan, who nobly agreed that he'd help me return to Bromley – four flights of stairs or not – I discharged myself. I'd been in hospital for nearly six months, I was becoming institutionalised and had to break the cycle. The staff weren't happy with the decision, but they understood how terrible it was for me, as a healthy person, to be trapped in a place in which all of the friends I'd made had already gone.

CHAPTER TWENTY-FOUR

What'll I Do?

A vicious frost cut the air as I wheeled out of hospital. Frightened and sad, I was too weak to walk. It had taken hours to pack the collected belongings of nearly six months' residence. I felt unsteady physically and emotionally, as if I was cutting myself off from a lifeline. Venturing out into a world I no longer knew anything about.

Andrew was away that day, visiting his father. I hadn't asked him to help. Duncan loaded the car, helped by his friend who'd been sharing our home in Bromley and helping out with the mortgage payments. We set off through the busy London traffic.

A romantic tape played in the car and I thought constantly of Andrew. Some acquaintances hadn't looked surprised when I told them I was worried about our relationship. They implied it was completely understandable if he was to finish with me. This hurt me deeply, slicing into my wounds of humiliation with a fresh blade. 'The poor man, having to put up with you Di, the way you are now – how could he be expected to?' This was not said, but implied. They understood how "poor" Andrew must be feeling. Even my mother expressed sympathies for him which put me at a new all-time low.

I felt terrible but more determined than ever to win his love back. I realised by now that he probably wanted to end the "relationship" – the majority of which had been conducted in a hospital, but hadn't been able to pluck up courage to do so. I couldn't believe that he actually would, though, so my fresh hope was that he'd been waiting until I was out of hospital to see how it would be out in the real world. We hadn't split up after all – I was still his girlfriend. Though I was heading for a home that was now entirely unsuitable for me, doing something nobody thought I would do, I sincerely carried this hope. If this isn't attempting to get back to normal I don't know what is, I said to myself. Surely, without all those hospital visits, all we needed were some good times together again in the real world. *Then* he would come to his senses and show some love for me.

Dear Dunky offered to carry me up the stairs but I refused. I painfully plodded my way up, aware of each false step, my phantom feet walking ahead of me, reminding me of how I used to fly up the carpeted tread. Duncan walked beside me. I'd only done minimal walking on parallel bars and a little around the wards at this stage. The chaffing of the prosthetics against my sore skin increased as we went but I was determined not to give in.

It took so long that we resorted to humming our way up one flight. He sang *True Love* thinking, I believe, that at last I had come to my senses and would be his.

My emotions were still so wrapped up with Andrew I didn't for a moment consider that Dunky might still want me back again. He had a girlfriend now and his actions were those of a good friend.

I hummed Irving Berlin's *What'll I Do?* a tune of lost love.

I stopped for a rest half way up, giving Becky and Gordon the shock of their lives when they opened their door.

Becky screamed. She couldn't believe it.

After an emotional reunion it was time to climb the last flight of stairs. Finally, we reached our front door at the top. I'd done it.

The door looked alien in its familiarity. To think it had been here all that time. Ever since…

Walking into the flat was strange too. The prosthetics were causing me quite severe pain now. I crumpled down onto the first chair I came to, the mis-matched splintered junk shop find at the dining table, and looked around. It was a shock. The homeliness of it – rooms without beds in them. The faint smell of cooking, garlic and coffee. Carpeted floors, sagging shelves piled with paperbacks. No corridors with nurses outside.

As soon as I got my breath back I called Andrew.

He was stunned.

I told him I needed time to unpack and settle in and he asked if he could come over at the weekend. I was happy with that. It gave me time to adjust to my new non-hospital persona – it was all happening just as I'd planned.

By the time Saturday came word had got around and friends were dropping in at all hours to wish me well. By the time Andrew arrived, the flat had taken on a bit of a permanent party atmosphere. Always happier in a crowd, he seemed pleased with that. Which pleased me. But when we were finally alone together he didn't come close to me. Instead he mumbled something about us being friends.

I felt myself going into shock, all energy draining from my body. Instead of comforting me he made for the door, turning and mouthing 'I love you' before literally running off into the night. I heard his heavy steps down every stair, and out into the street, clumping his way to freedom on those rain-splattered streets.

Everything hit me at once. I was (quietly) hysterical. The total reality of my situation dawned on me for the first time. I had been completely delusional. I could perceive my body had changed but I hadn't changed inside.

Duncan was out with some friends and I was completely alone. It was one of the worst nights of my life that'd had quite a few really bad nights in it already over the previous months. I pulled myself into the wheelchair and made my way to the kitchen where I ran my hands under the cold water tap, over and over.

Duncan's knife set lay on the counter. Briefly, I admired the steel perfection of his chef's tools and thought of the surgeons who had saved my life. I picked the smallest one up and held it briefly to my wrist. No. I put it back down again.

I dropped into full on reality. When Duncan returned, and I had phoned the nearest friend, Sue, I sat there, catatonic with grief. They phoned the emergency GP's number. He came over, tutted at my tale of woe, relayed by Sue, and gave me some antidepressants. I took one but woke at 5am with the sensation of wasps buzzing in my head. I put the drugs in the bin.

Duncan was quietly supportive but his quiet whistling tunes around the flat relayed what he was really thinking. I realise now that everybody was probably quite pleased. They could see how Andrew had been treating me. He should have had the balls to finish with me in hospital, surrounded by professional carers. But the real, deep grief came about because everybody understood why Andrew had backed off. "Who wouldn't do the same in Andrew's situation?" was the consensus. And it was expected that I would understand that. I didn't at the time. I didn't at all. I felt very, very bad.

'Free will, Di. You can't go against free will,' my sister said. Even my mum…

I understood it was a terrible position for Andrew to be put in but the mortal hurt complimented the physical hurt. I was very glad Duncan was there. I moved back into the main bedroom, conceded to him when we'd split up. There, a new surprise encounter lay waiting for me. My old wardrobe, crammed with all my clothes.

Every item from bum-hugging jeans to short cocktail dresses ignited sparks of grief. I ran my fingertips down the materials, each texture reminding me of a body that no longer existed.

As soon as I could I picked them out in handfuls and handed them to my friend Sue. We'd been a similar size.

'I can't Di. I couldn't wear them.' She shook her head. Dead man's shoes is a phrase that comes to mind. She took them with her but never wore them. Who'd want to be reminded of me?

The world was a dark place indeed stuck inside that back bedroom up those four flights of stairs. I felt like Rapunzel. With much shorter hair.

CHAPTER TWENTY-FIVE

Solitaire

All the laughter that had done so much to help me through my hospital days had gone. I felt trapped and hemmed in. Delusions shattered, I struggled through the onset of clinical reality as best I could. I knew the time had come for me to get real now and face whatever future I had, however bleak, square on and alone.

My main preoccupation, securing a partner to love and to share a loving life with, had gone. An interesting facet of being single in my situation is that one has to wait and see who comes forward. Previously if I saw a man I fancied the attraction game would start. That had all gone now. I was in passive mode. Infirm. Who'd ever want me?

Instead, I poured all my hopes for the future into work. I continued working part-time, as I'd been doing in hospital, but wanted to get back to the office as soon as possible. For this to work on any regular basis I'd have to come down from my Rapunzel Tower and find accessible, ground floor accommodation close to our Wandsworth office on the other side of town. A major dilemma to which there was no quick solution.

The extent of the lack of control over my own life was a big shock. Friends of course would come frequently to help me down to the ground and out into the world, but these gestures only exacerbated a different tangent to my dilemma. I had to gracefully accept whatever I was offered. Refusing arrangements made in advance was difficult if, when the time came, I wasn't feeling up to it. It was pointless to be grumpy to those closest to me so I bottled it up. This repressed frustration at others' kindnesses made me feel worse than ever.

More than a little fear was involved. Dealing with the external world on my new legs made every outing a challenge. Every time, to this day, before I step outside the door I have to do a damage assessment. How long am I going to be out? Is drinking involved? How am I going to go to the loo? The potential for danger, for toppling over on an alien surface, for the sheer inability to react quickly, was everywhere. Any tiny little thing on the floor was enough to fell me. Sometimes I'd find myself literally frozen to the spot. This happened on one of my early training excursions from the hospital to The Depot, a lovely riverside restaurant in Barnes. I walked from the car to the entrance with no problems but couldn't lift my foot over the threshold of the doorway. I became literally paralysed with fear.

Social occasions, too, were now fraught with new difficulties. It's one thing to be stuck with the party bore, another when you have no smooth, quick way of extricating yourself out of the situation. Even worse would be the pain vultures, the types who can't get enough of bad news and come to feed off your pain. In an unaware, subconscious way of course, most of them, but it doesn't make it any easier to deal with or to get away from.

'You will get back to doing most of what you did before but it's going to take a long, long time, Di.' The words of my physioterrorist haunted me day and night. I'd dismissed her at the time. She didn't know the power of my strength and resolve.

I spent Christmas in the aching bosom of my family.

My father's fall had pushed the back of his neck into his spine, temporarily paralysing him down one side. Caring for him was a full-time job for my mum and I knew I couldn't add to her burden by moving home as well, even if I'd wanted to. Perhaps that was a blessing in disguise for me. However difficult it was proving to get my old city life back, the option of moving home for good wasn't something that ever needed to be discussed between us.

We moved on autopilot through the traditional Christmas festivities in the most untraditional circumstances. The emotions most on our minds (Oh Christ, we've become a "tragic" family) were never discussed. They vibrated under the surface of all our faces and all our actions. We were stiff upper lip en masse.

Conversations revolved around the now and the future, avoiding all mention of the most recent past. There were constant hugs and kisses but little eye contact. We all feared to acknowledge the grief sketched across our eyes. Sustained eye contact would have produced tears and possibly a downward spiral into grief from which we may never have rallied. We were a tragic family now. Two healthy people, my dad and I, in a family of five had been severely disabled in a matter of weeks.

One evening Dad and I sat watching the moving colour on the TV, both of our own thought patterns running riot through the past.

'Dad,' I asked. 'Don't you think it's strange that both of us have been so severely injured within weeks of each other?'

He mused for an instant. Then replied, 'No sweetie. Whole families are wiped out in car crashes. Statistics. That's all.' Sensible, wise, that was my dad. I looked at him and tears came to my eyes. At least he was still with us.

Worse than Christmas, New Year's Eve loomed. For many those three little words can strike social fear into the heart of even the most fun-loving spirit.

Why? So much hope is placed at the door of New Year's Eve, especially if you are single, and particularly if you are recently bereaved as I was that New Year's Eve.

My God I'd dreaded that particular night on countless occasions. The overblown build-up, the pressure to be somewhere exciting in the run up to the cruel hands of time ticking off those precious 12 seconds – but none more so than that year. I was legless before I'd even sniffed a bottle of bubbly.

Previous New Year evening plans had included glamorous dinner parties – hours of preparation with too much make up and not enough clothing. Have you ever wandered the streets after midnight on New Year's Eve looking for something special – a lasting atmosphere, an indication from God that this is indeed a very special night – in a mini-dress and no coat? And always at midnight, that dreadful kissing of people you'd think twice about shaking hands with in the cold light of day? Followed by the anti-climactic "that's it". What have I done over the last year? What have I achieved? Bugger all. That's what. In fact I went into 1991 in the minus – two big minuses, with the losses piling up slowly all around me. Minus two legs. Minus one handsome boyfriend. Minus one beautiful home. And a previously glowing career that now looked a bit rocky – half a minus.

You may be thinking that I was feeling sorry for myself. You'd be wrong. Despair threatened at any second to erupt and then to submerge me forever more in the pit of mental hell, but I never allowed the potential for self-pity to erupt. Grief gnawed away inside, like a hidden disease, an emotional cancer. I was afraid that if I allowed any dismal thoughts to develop outwards it would produce a lumpy bitterness. A hatred for the world that I simply didn't feel. I kept it under control by adhering to an old maxim – "get on with life" – and tried not to allow myself time to dwell on the agony that raged inside.

For there was agony – physical and emotional. A cynical bitterness would spark inside my tortured head, illuminating the dreadful ironies of life. For in fact I had achieved something in the latter half of that fateful year. A fame of sorts. An enduring New Year's resolution I had made to myself every year since I could remember, in secret, as the bells chimed in London, in the Cheshire of my childhood, and abroad. That I would be known for something. I always felt it would be work-based. I was wrong.

I had been heralded as the Fall Girl in the *Today* newspaper (great journalism – shame that newspaper closed down). I had superseded news on the Gulf war to head up the front page in the Press. I had been discussed in Parliament. I had been the "must tell" news topic among the 500 or so people who had visited me in hospital. I was known to thousands of people. 15 minutes of sickening fame. A victim of accident. A victim in life. I would not be discussed (and boy, were my ears burning) without a shake of the head, a tut tut on the breath, a tear in the eye and a "there but for the grace of God go I". I had secured a living epitaph – The Woman With No Legs. Not so many of them knew I now also had the mother of all battles on my hands to prove my innocence. To prove I hadn't brought this upon myself. To prove I wasn't a lying, scheming trespasser out for what I could get. Thankfully I didn't yet know myself the extent of the battle ahead. A fight that would be more distressing than anything I'd yet gone through in my entire life.

CHAPTER TWENTY-SIX

How Deep Is Your Love?

Along with the Christmas Cards had come a thick, beige envelope with the now familiar Coopers crest.

This reminder of the oncoming legal fight chilled but there was some good news at least. Stan Hall, the railway safety expert, had completed his preliminary investigations. His report made it clear that if correct emergency protocol been followed, the train should have stopped after 60 feet (18 metres) and had that been the case I most probably wouldn't have gone under the tracks at all.

If, as the ticket collector claimed, the train had been moving when I'd crossed the footbridge and was at the top of the stairs, I would never have reached it, let alone the last door of the fourth carriage. If the train had started moving as I reached the platform, the acceleration and braking distances wouldn't match the train's stop position. So, technically speaking, our expert witness has come to the conclusion that he thinks the train had to be stationary when I attempted to board.

If the guard were to have shouted and acted immediately, hitting the stop bell or the emergency brake, or if the driver responded immediately, then, going on Mr Hall's expert knowledge of average acceleration and braking distance, the train should have stopped at less than half the distance than it did.

So that means either the guard wasn't aware I was there and thus negligent. Or he was aware that I was there and for some reason delayed in acting. So whether the train was moving or not is actually irrelevant. The train didn't stop soon enough regardless.

As I said, this was all good news for our case. But good news can sometimes be hard to bear.

I lay in bed that night looking at the metallic structure of the wheelchair pressed up against the side of the bed. My gaze drifted to the two prosthetic limbs leaning in the corner of the bedroom. My dear mum had been so determined to empathise with my new body that I had encouraged her to try on the below knee leg. She pushed and pushed with her foot to try to get it on...We cried with laughter when both of us realised this just wasn't possible. I could not bear the grief that I had laid on my parents, my close friends, my family were suffering so deeply. Was this really me? Was this really my life now? I craved a feeling of normality, a semblance of the regular pattern of life. It came in the form of my diaries which my brother David found in the attic. He gave them to me, smiling.

I turned onto my side, all disabled equipment out of sight, and focussed on the diaries. They detailed my life from the mid-70s through to the mid-80s. A large page-a-day that listed the average nuances of regular schoolgirl, university, first job activity. Recurring themes kept popping up – lack of boys, then as I got older, lack of men. Late teenage angst, arrogance, ranting against the injustices of the world. Job worries, but also the shiny, if brief, glories. A first date. A new friend. Rushes of adrenaline when a new job had been secured. All these events paled into insignificance compared with what I was now having to deal with.

Looking back like this on my life as it was lived before the accident was a significant moment. Two events especially made me think long and hard about the cruel tricks and happy accidents that happen along the way to all of us in some shape or form. The first was the manner in which I lost my virginity. All my girlfriends had passed through this moment at the ages of 15/16 or so. I was more than ready to join them, and listened to their blow by blow accounts with complete, and ever-growing, envy, accompanied, more often than not, by third party horror – so unromantic and sordid were some of their tales. But it wasn't to be for me until I was nearly twenty and a whole year of university life had already been lived. The three years previous to me losing my cherry had been fraught with mostly "disaster" scenarios but when I finally succumbed, my first full sexual experience was with an Australian cricketer who I had first met when I was 16, where I shyly got just his autograph. Three years later I met up with him again, and spent a few days at the Waldorf Hotel in London. It was a "dream come true" – incredible. Fantasy had become reality! As sections from those diaries reveal...

August 1976

Bless you Daddy for introducing me to the wonderful world of cricket! Today, at Headingley I MET Jeff Thomson, god, he is so gorgeous. Got his autograph, nobody else did. Even more smitten now. Oh, why don't I live in Australia? ....

August 1980

Do things happen "for a reason"? I cannot believe what has come about over the last week of my life. All that distress, three years of pining for boys/men that came to nothing... so strange that I should pop my cherry with the total fantasy dreamboat that is JT.

Being taken back to this angst of that time made me realise how life really does have its strange ways of working out for the best sometimes. It was a powerful additional feeling of strength – a feeling that life sometimes works out OK. Over time, and with patience – and humour.

The other was to see how desperately unhappy I'd been about getting my first pair of contact lenses. These were the days before soft lenses – and they were rock hard. Wearing them felt just like having your eyeballs scratched out all day long, until you got used to them. I was intrigued to see how much I hated them but how I was determined to persevere because of the promise they provided: freedom from having to wear detested specs ever again. So though my whole body reacted against them, I refused to give up because I was desperate to be able to see without glasses. It wasn't just the vanity, it was everything about them, the way they slipped off your face, the way rain got in the way. The way you had to store them in ugly, boxy old lady cases that snapped shut. The alternative, though, felt so much worse at first. A physical invasion of my body. It was funny to read how conflicted I felt. I could apply those feelings wholly to the legs. I applied the same brain pattern. They were what was necessary if I was to get any semblance of independence again. I simply had to learn to get used to them if I didn't want to live the rest of my life at crotch level. (Interesting as this can be though, at times.)

Patience, a characteristic previously unknown to me, had now been forced upon me. I'd been someone who'd felt that time was too precious to leave to patience. I pondered this irony when I went to call upon a friend I'd known since early school days. She'd moved to a new house and the garden was covered in building rubble. As I picked my way so carefully over the bricks and heaps of old wood, I thought this is what I am having to do. Be patient and I will get there. And it was going to be worth it.

Ceri, her pretty pussy cat face smiling from the doorstep called out. 'Come on Diana. You can do it. If you make it without falling over there's the promise of a French fancy and one of Uncle Bert's pickled onions!'

It was comments like these that made the struggle worth it, I thought as I finally stepped over Ceri's threshold.

Patience and humour worked again when Helen and I went to meet up with another old friend – Karen, who was nine months pregnant.

We met in a pub that we'd frequented as three teenage girls on the pull – and laughed at the thought of our hair (splattered with gold streaks from a gold paint can), clothes (tight trousers in fake leopard print – lovely!) and make-up (heavy on the kohl and blusher, really heavy on the lip-gloss). 'We didn't pull very often did we?' We all agreed. We were giggling over past exploits so much that I forgot how much I was drinking. Not that I was worried about alcoholic content. I was supping lager shandies – watching the amount, for it meant the dreaded trip to the loo. And public loos were now potentially difficult places for me to go.

They are:

1. Often upstairs or downstairs. I had to go slowly. Would my bladder make it in time?

2. Often tiny places, with no room to swing a ballcock – would I fit in?

3. Once inside, could I reliably lean on the walls to get me down onto the loo seat and hoist myself up again (I was still haunted by that shopping trip and the flimsy changing room walls falling down).

Anyway, a girl's got to go. My bladder control was now in superb nick, but all those shandies, all that giggling. Karen and I made our way to the loo which was thankfully on the same level and big enough to swing a ballcock in. Nine months preggie, she moved her way round like a magnificent ship. It was her third child and she presented it all out front, like a grocer with his counter laden with goodies. Once inside the cubicle, I swung and slunk myself into position, holding onto the walls on my way down to the seat below. And a long way down it seemed to me. It was, a recent import to UK décor from the European furniture shows: a LOW-SLUNG LOO. And it was too late. I was on it. After I'd relieved myself, I found I couldn't get off it.

'Karen,' I asked feebly. 'Have you done, love?'

'Yes,' she giggled. 'Why?'

'It's just that I think I need a bit of a hoist to get me off this bloody loo.' I leaned forward as far as I dared and undid the loo door. Karen appeared in front of me. Well, her tummy did. That's all that would fit into the cubicle. Luckily, nature had smiled on us in one way. Karen has beautifully long legs and arms and she now put her upper body to good use, grappling me off, up, and, eventually, out. Any embarrassment on my part was entirely wiped out by our laughter.

And it was laughter and love from friends that got me through New Year's Eve. As the day drew closer I was saved by a phone call from Dinah, who lived in Little Neston on the Wirral. She asked Helen and I over to bring in the new year with her family and our dear Brookside actor friend Paul Usher.

Dinah set the scene beautifully for that first New Year's Eve in my different body by telling me, as I delicately made my way to her comfortable sofa, that I looked slender and lovely. 'You look like your old self, Di,' she declared. 'When I think back to how we all felt when you were first in hospital, and now, only months later – look at you!' Adding, in her giving, empathetic way, 'A movie star in red!'

Paul further added to my confidence by capturing my sole attention for the whole evening. He and I moved to the quieter dining room as the party room filled up. With odd interruption of guests offering drinks and nibbles, we stared at each other, his eyes reading mine.

'Your eyes have changed,' he said. 'I can see the pain. It's not unattractive.'

He grabbed one of Taki's guitars and sang songs for me. To me. Enveloping me with a wistful happiness. Restoring a belief that I could be attractive. Another friend to add to those I will love forever.

Travelling back with Helen along the silent motorway at four in the morning, I felt different. Some emotional change had taken place. I didn't feel so internally wretched. There was a glimmer of hope that life could be reasonable. That my scale of emotional experience could rise above the decibel of grief.

A few days later I had to go back into hospital for a couple of nights. Climbing up and down the stairs at home had damaged the skin graft on my right leg.

I didn't exactly have a spring in my step when I finally returned to work a few days later but a sense of quiet purpose had been restored. Helen picked me up from Bromley, helped me down the four sets of stairs and drove me to Wandsworth.

We passed Wandsworth Common station. I felt physically sick. My heart rippled extra beats and I had to breathe very deeply to steady myself. The accident replayed itself at top speed through my brain. Flickers of memory so far unremembered caught me unawares. I could smell the hot day, I could feel my mutilated body being laid onto the stretcher. I heard the whispered tones of those around me. The voices of compassion as they slid me into the cool air of the ambulance. And all the while Helen drove, up over the station road bridge. Sweat trickled at my forehead. This wasn't a good idea. I was thinking I shouldn't be going anywhere near this area of London. What other memories were going to be thrown into my consciousness, to batter and bruise my highly vulnerable mind? The feeling accelerated as I walked my slow walk to the door of Sarah's home – MediaVision's office.

I stared at the house, in particular the door: its green paintwork, its round brassy door knocker. I made my way up the steps and turned to wave Helen goodbye. My hand enclosed around the knocker and I was momentarily hypnotised. This was what I had pulled to close the door on that final day. It was the last contact I'd experienced with something fixed and solid in my "previous life". I held onto it as if grasping for some sort of energy. Willing the past six months to be wiped out, for it all to have been a nightmare, and now, finally, I was going to wake up.

Sarah opened the door, smiling sweetly. We hugged and she led me to the dining room where she had laid out a temporary office. I opened the post and we talked about projects, all aimed to re-boot the company after its hiatus. Sarah had done a valiant job keeping the company ticking over, but potential clients were clearly waiting to gauge my progress before they committed any PR contracts to us. We were a team. A partnership had been sold to them previous to the accident and that was still what most of them wanted. There was a meeting in town but I was feeling a bit shell shocked and rather weary. We agreed Sarah should go on her own, and start spreading the good news that I was officially "back at work". She went to change into a smart business suit and when she returned all I could see was her beauty. Her figure, her face, her mobility, the swing of the handbag on her shoulder, the car keys in her hand.

'Should I make coffee before I go?' she asked.

I can't even make a cup of coffee and carry it, I thought. I began to sob. Sarah came to me, hugging me close to her. 'Please I want to be beautiful again. Please,' I begged, my body wracking with pain, huddling into my business partner's arms.

I was pleading for the past. That sense when you wish you could repeat an earlier experience now extended itself to the whole of my previous life. The grass was certainly greener in my memory. All the grass of my original existence was the greenest, sweetest type you could imagine. And yet – I knew what I had to do. I resolutely refused to be a victim. I was a survivor. These types of thoughts didn't actually go through my head at the time. It is pure sub-conscious that develops this type of process.

What I knew I had to do was to work my way through it, break the emotional pain barriers, as I'd done with the physical pain barriers to wear the false limbs. I was taking the emotional pain head-on.

In hindsight I can see that it was for these reasons that I stayed working at the company I had set up before the accident; why I had moved back to my previous home, and then, later, lived in a home so close to the train station where the catastrophe had occurred.

Some people change the rest of their lives when something major has happened. I could have done that, but I was bound up in a type of duty: to Sarah with regard to the company; and to family and friends in a determination that I was going to be alright. It's a type of arrogance, a personality trait of the survivor.

I certainly needed survival tactics to cope with the type of situation I was now enduring. I used to fly out of bed in the mornings. I could be up and out on my way to work in ten minutes. It now took me an hour and a half every morning. The diminishment of stamina means I have to carefully plan where my energies have to go. PR involves a lot of running around. Networking is what it's all about, darting around, working the room at parties, introducing people. Long-term, the biggest and most traumatic loss of all is this loss of energy, but I didn't know that then, and certainly wouldn't have accepted it if I had. I was trying desperately to do it all. To be as I was before.

A routine of sorts was set up – and this was just what I probably needed after such an upheaval. I would rise early. Helen or Sarah would collect me and take me to the office where I would work solidly until evening, and then, energy levels willing, would go out in the evening with friends, who, bless them, were still showing an active interest in my welfare.

Due to our contract with RPTA/Primetime, another problem was having to meet up again with Andrew on a fairly regular basis. I would make an extra effort with my appearance and would try desperately to instil nonchalance into my painful steps as I tip-tapped my way down the long Primetime corridor. Andrew would suddenly appear, his eyes slightly wild, his aura exuding guilt. He would lunge at me, kiss my cheek, his voice both husky with too many cigarettes and then pitched high, as he would ask how I was, without waiting for a proper reply. Not that I ever gave him one. Everything was always "great". MediaVision would be doing "very well" and I, for all the world, would look as if I'd won the the jackpot in Vegas, so fixed was the smile. It was an Oscar-winning performance. And everyone just about believed it. Including me. More importantly, it worked. "Pretending" to be feeling alright about the world on my face, so flirtatious were my hands as I hugged and kissed everyone I saw. "See, look!" I would force my body language to say. "Diana's back! She may walk a little bit funny, but she's still the same old Di! Nothing has changed really."

It actually got me through. I would frequently reel in grief as I left the Primetime building, blinded by tears, the mask of pretence broken, and would weep all the way home, but only Sarah was witness to this.

CHAPTER TWENTY-SEVEN

You've Got A Friend (s)

One night when I didn't have to put on any pretence of feeling reasonable with life was the Benefit Evening. Organised by Annie Keavency, an actress I'd met on *Brookside*, it involved two other actors from the same soap putting on a special performance of a two hander play, at the Young Vic. Sue Johnston (Sheila Grant in *Brookie*) and John McCardle (Billy Corkhill) were the actors.

Their stunning performance was followed by an auction of goodies collected by Annie and Sarah and the actors themselves. TV stars Pauline Quirke and Linda Robson turned up – Annie had been in *Birds of a Feather* – buckets swinging in their hands, cajoling the audience of over 300 people for donations.

I was simply overwhelmed – by the support, the generosity, the kindness of spirit of that evening, but most of all for making me feel so special and valued. When Annie stood up to make a speech and finished with the words, 'and I have never seen courage like it,' tears pricked at my eyes and I beamed with pride. People stood up to give me a standing ovation. Then I stood up to thank them and was shaking so much as I rose, I nearly fell over. I turned it into a joke and thanked people from the depth of my heart, for that is where they had touched me. Their combined efforts had raised my spirit far and above any type of experience I'd ever had in my whole life.

It couldn't have come at a better time. Middle of February – snow on the ground – and my energy levels at an all time low. I felt recharged and convinced that I was doing OK. The £4,000 (around $5,900) raised was an added, but much-needed, bonus.

Andrew had been there. In the gloom of the theatre light, I sensed that he was watching me, almost wistfully. For once I felt in control of my emotional situation. I flirted with everyone – men and women, and in particular my male gay friends who I felt particularly close to. A minority, talked about, teased, a difficult card in life to have drawn, gay people are forced to feel different, as if it's anybody's business what type of sexuality one wishes to follow. Judgmental attitudes prevail in our society – principally based on fear of the unknown, the lack of ability to feel empathy.

I was my own worst enemy when I decided to judge myself in the eyes of others. Keeping my business as usual flag flying high, I decided that I'd be going to Cannes, my second home, that April for my first television market since the accident.

I'd actually only missed one market – in October – and people were fairly stunned, that I should travel abroad so soon, and to such a destination. I was determined to prove however that MediaVision was back in business. Big-style. I was happy to see my old friends and acquaintances, but deeply distressed at my changed circumstances. My determination to keep up my front and not to use the wheelchair except in the hotel became a struggle. But I thought a necessary one.

Public relations in such a glamorous setting is based, sadly, on a superficial view. Sarah and I had exploited the combination of our attractiveness before the accident, and part of me longed to do the same again. We were the working Princesses – Diana and Sarah, without the HRH. I felt awkward and that it would be better if people did not associate me with a wheelchair. I walked the miles around the exhibition stands, smiling through the pain, being patted on the back, kissed on the cheek, lauded for my "courage", "bravery" and general stoicism. The comments gave me energy, confidence and prickles of pride that were to become part of my personality.

Max, my married ex-lover, took me out for a stunning dinner. We had enjoyed many such meals previously. Sex would normally have been part of the atmosphere between us. But not this time. I was more concerned with the expense of the food we were consuming and asked the waiter for a "poche du chien" (doggy bag) for the petits fours we couldn't manage. I'd always had a social conscience at the very different lives people have to live, had been dismayed at the severe chasms between the "haves" and the "have-nots" in this world. This sense of injustice had, since my accident, grown quite substantially. Pre-accident, I'd tell people off in my bossy way if they started to moan about being in Cannes. How hot it was, how hard they were having to work.

'Look around you!' I'd say. 'What a beautiful place to be able to work. You're lucky!'

So what happened now was that when discussing anything they deemed as "trivial" with me they would express their guilt and shut up. A part of me missed these superficial conversations. The removal of petty talk of clothes, shoes, boyfriend worries, whinges about work, took away another great chunk of normality from my life.

Though being with Max reminded me of how much I missed sex, I couldn't think of anyone who I wanted to make love with. I was probably also giving off the vibes of someone not confident enough to express themselves sexually. I hadn't lost the gift of flirtation but there was something within me holding back.

This was compounded by William, a journalist mate who worked at the *Hollywood Reporter*, asking to stay in the small spare bed in my hotel room. It wasn't discussed, but I knew that should he have to tell his girlfriend where he'd stayed on his first night in Cannes, he'd only have to explain WHO he was staying with and there would be no cause for jealousy, or suspicion, to be raised in her mind.

At the age of thirty I was being viewed as a non-sexual person by other people around me. There was one horribly awkward moment when an attractive man came to sit opposite me as I waited for Sarah in the Majestic bar. By the eye contact he was clearly interested in the way I looked. And then I got up to welcome Sarah and his face dropped to the floor as he saw me pick up the two walking sticks. I was deeply hurt and have never forgotten that sudden change in facial expression.

Andrew's attitude at the benefit night and his apparent continued interest in me prompted me to ask him out for a drink. We met in a pub near his work. The scene of our original courtship when we would snog our way through a lunchtime and return to his office, flush-cheeked and buoyed up with drinks and lust. I was as nervous as hell when he strode in, giving me a cursory kiss on the forehead and flinging his motorbike gloves on the table. Part of me longed for him to remember me as I had been, as it all had been, and that we could start again and pretend that our parting hadn't come in the most extreme of circumstances. But it wasn't to be. He was pleased I was doing well but was distracted. He even looked pissed off that he was the one who had to continually go to the bar to replenish the drinks.

I'd asked Helen and her boyfriend, Jonny to pick me up, and he looked so relieved when they turned up. He'd invited his two best friends – Susan and John – as his form of "protection", underlining the fact that in his mind we could only ever be friends. The evening took an even worse dimension when John suddenly started to cry, and wouldn't stop. I hugged him, a physical embrace of an apology for making him feel so bad, although frankly I was embarrassed, having this grown man weeping on me in a pub. He whispered in my ear, 'Andrew did love you, you know'. And then kept repeating the same phrase over and over. 'It was more than duty, it was more than duty.'

Helen and Jonny whisked me away from the trauma. I didn't cry in the car. I was silent and they let me be so. When we got to Bromley, Helen saw me up the stairs and loved and hugged the life out of me when we got to the top.

'You will do much better Di, please believe it.'

'Can you fathom it out at all Helga?' I began to sob. (She's good on philosophy.)

'It's free will that's all. Andrew exercised his right to free will.'

I cried for about five minutes. Then, over a cup of tea, I suddenly stopped. A strength that had been given as a gift to me in hospital, restored. Part of this strength was also a kind of anger. I was very angry that Andrew had made ME feel so awkward, guilty and ashamed because of what had happened to me.

'Weak shites, the lot of them,' I concluded and never cried for Andrew again.

CHAPTER TWENTY-EIGHT

There's A Ghost In My House (and it's me)

After so much work, I needed a holiday. In my previous life I would have rung around a few companies, secured the best deal for my chosen area – Greece, or perhaps Greece, or, occasionally, Greece, packed a bag and raced to the airport with time for a quick swing around the Duty Free shops. I would return looking tanned and feeling refreshed and recharged in order to fling myself at another work project, another lover.

This time was clearly going to be different. With close friends Jane and Sue, I would be hiring a villa. I spent hours on the phone debating with strangers the door widths of villas in Portugal, the steps in Spain and the accessibility to swimming pools in Tenerife. Facilities for the disabled weren't on the public conscience at all at that time. I was driven to "confess" to my new body on the phone and waited for the responses which ranged from: "oh poor you", to a sensible silence as I scored doodles of closed boxes into my note pad.

Suitable villa secured, a girl's mind turns to holiday clothing. Sue came shopping with me to Bromley. Foolhardy, and clearly still in denial, I left the wheelchair at home and walked my equivalent of the marathon to the shops. I leaned heavily into Sue who held one of my sticks and I clung onto her arm, feeding off the strength of her body to support my own.

In a department store I finally admitted defeat and, sweating and out of breath, sat heavily on some suitcases piled high in a promotion for the store. I ignored the glares from the staff and looked around to see a woman in an electric wheelchair, with a baby cocooned in a papoose snuggled on her front. I am ashamed to say I stared and stared. At that moment I wanted what she had. I wanted her gliding, stopping and starting chair which seemed to hover over the floor and, most of all, I wanted someone to love me enough to give me a baby like the delicious child cuddled close to her, moving his head slightly back so that he could get eye contact with the most important person in his world.

She skimmed and burred her way up to me and stared back, her eyes blazing. To her I must have seemed like the typical bored shopper – staring at her because she was "different". She'd looked genuinely content, one arm cradling her child, the other operating her mode of transport, her eyes glazed as they took in the mass of goods presented in the shop. And I'd ruined it, my staring had pierced her temporary bubble of contentment.

She couldn't see my sticks which had fallen behind the suitcases. She couldn't know that concealed beneath my trousers were two legs made of fibreglass and metal. I opened my mouth to apologise, but it would have meant almost yelling to her to explain my apparent rudeness. I put my head down to look for my sticks. By the time I'd got up to approach her to say that what she'd taken for rampant curiosity and displaced pity was actually envy and admiration, it was too late. As I hoisted myself off the suitcase she circled and jolted her chair into jogging speed to get out of the store and away from my gaze as quickly as possible.

I haven't ventured out on a long shopping trip without my wheelchair since then.

Becky joined us from her flat below, having left her beautiful baby in the care of Gordon, her husband. Quickly I lifted my jacket, blouse and bra off to try on one of the sexy tops I had bought. Subconsciously I was clearly willing to expose as much of my bosom as possible. "nice tits, shame about the legs" rang through my head.

I squeezed my breasts together and sucked in my cheeks hard. A pose from the previous Diana. Becky and Sue laughed and suggested I try on the matching trousers. This threw me off balance. Why did I feel OK about exposing my breasts to close girlfriends and not my lower half? I shrugged and carefully took off my trousers, revealing the thick leather belt that held on the above knee leg and then, as I pulled the trousers down further the white plastic and the unnatural tan of the prosthetic stockings. I scrabbled for the new clothes and stood up from the wheelchair to pull them over the false feet. Sue played with some tissue. Becky stood, hands on hips, and looked.

'If you don't mind me saying Di, you've still got a beautiful body. Lovely skin.' Perhaps I should have minded at the word "still" but I didn't. I smiled at her.

'Very sexy you know, Di.'

'Are you turning lezzie on me Becks? Eh? Now you've got your baby, had enough of men eh?'

We had a bit of a chuckle. I looked in a full-length mirror. Something I rarely did. If I didn't move, stood as still as a photographic model, I looked good. Perhaps the old Diana was there posing away, I mused, just as long as I stood as still as a statue.

The holiday was, overall, a great success and notched me still further up and away from the baseline of grief. My research into the holiday destination paid off handsomely – the villa was perfect for a wheelchair user. Most of the seven days were spent around and in the swimming pool where, because one of my legs is longer than the other, I swam around in circles until I got the hang of it. The sensation of being in the water was utter heaven to my damaged body. The water seemed to soothe my limbs which were finally – after nine months – free to move as they had before. I would launch myself up onto the lilo and lie floating on the lilting water, looking up at the clouds, fingertips in the water, acknowledging the nudges of happiness that had so far eluded me.

It wasn't all plain sailing. Jane and Sue left early one morning to potter around the local market in search of fresh strawberries and sardines. I lay by the pool, reading with false concentration, for in the new silence I was aware of my total aloneness in a strange environment, and that if anything untoward should happen, how would I raise the alarm? The villa was at the end of a long steep track, difficult enough to manoeuvre in a car, impossible to walk in the false limbs. Panic and paranoia ate their way into my head and I dashed for the bedroom and dried off, putting the limbs on as quickly as possible. I was trying to instil a little control into my situation, without success.

Jane and Sue found me one hour later still in the bedroom, silently crying with frustration. The above knee mechanism had locked in the heat, clicking the long leg straight out in front of me, like a plaster cast on a broken leg. I'd stripped the prosthetic cover off, and was fiddling with the basic wiring when they burst into the room, arms laden with fruit, veg and flowers.

'It was lovely, you must come tomorrow Di...' their voices broke off when they saw my tears and the state of my leg. I blamed my crying on the leg, keeping hidden from them that it was only a symptom of the real cause of distress. The uncontrollable fear that had taken hold in their absence. I fixed the wiring with ease once their presence had calmed me down and began to acknowledge that the paranoia, the gross anxiety I had suffered at their absence was another side-effect of the accident. A type of post traumatic stress. Once acknowledged, it can be worked on, teasing and coaxing my own brain, my own emotions to be calm, to force a type of mental relaxation.

We all ventured out to the market the next day. The effects of sun and exercise on my body were producing contradictory results. All the relaxation and sunshine brought a tremendous sense of well-being. But also severe phantom pains, particularly in my feet – nightmare sensations, like feeling my missing toenails being extracted one by one, and phantom electric shocks which made my residual legs jump. This is where I had the bizarre experience of walking away from myself. As I stood on a pavement to cross a road I moved the false legs nearer to the kerb and waited for a car to pass. I looked up and saw Jane and Sue on the other side of the road, waiting. The kerb was higher than I realised, but I was determined to step down unaided except for my walking sticks. I moved the sticks into a position to lessen the jolt down into the gutter. I suddenly froze. My original body, present only in my mind, stepped down into the road for me, ahead of me, one phantom limb followed by the other, a quick, sure elegant action of old. I was left, gasping in reality on the pavement.

I was haunted by my own body. It's only the brain not accepting what has happened I kept telling myself – carrying out an action that it had done many millions of times before. But why? Why would my brain not accept what my heart and soul were beginning to acknowledge, and to live with?

Difficult moments aside, the holiday in Portugal proved to be yet another turning point in my emotional recovery. Jane, Sue and I had shared many laughs and the wonderful warmth that companionship on a successful holiday can produce. We all love the type of laughter that comes from the belly, wiping tears from your eyes, the helpless stuttering of words barely spoken, the exhaustion that leaves one feeling very content. I returned to London with the thoughts that life was becoming more "normal", with a more natural flow of peaks and troughs, rather than the severe chasms I had felt until then.

Certainly events began to move into place to speed up the "normality" process. But several major obstacles still stood in my way. Work was buzzing but increasingly exhausting; the court case, with all its uncertainties, was looming; and though, at last, it looked like a suitable ground floor flat had been found – how could I live all alone?

I approached each challenge head-on and, whilst not striding through them, I hobbled on in my own way. By the end of June I was installed in a ground floor flat in Tooting, south-west London, and driving my own car.

CHAPTER TWENTY-NINE

Drive

My new home in Elmbourne Road, London SW17 was a ground floor conversion of an old, brown-brick Victorian terrace that almost overlooked Tooting Common. The Common was the most desirable part of Tooting – least-awful is probably a better way of putting it. Tooting was one of those shabby areas of London described by estate agents at the time as up and coming. And they weren't wrong, Tooting did, eventually become a highly desirable, cool, part of town. But that wouldn't happen for a few decades yet.

Like many less salubrious parts of London, it was, at least, friendly, I was on the ground at last and it was convenient for both work and the hospital. I was, though, highly nervous about moving to the ground floor and in much reduced circumstances. Duncan valiantly agreed not only to live with me but to sleep on a sofa-bed in the living room. This meant we could rent out the Bromley flat to cover the mortgage payments.

The disabled facilities had been installed in the most depressing way imaginable. Enormous bright blue plastic stickers were stuck on everything, with a wheelchair symbol, just to remind me. Even the trolley had a "cup of tea" sticker to tell me that it was to place my tea on. I tried very hard not to use the wheelchair which meant the surfaces in the kitchen would then be too low, but day to day life did generally become a lot easier.

The previous tenant had been a wheelchair-user. Her widower, who'd stayed on for quite a while after she'd died until he could be re-housed, had left it in a terrible mess. We set to, removing all the horrible blue stickers and exorcising the atmosphere of poverty, smelly dog, sadness and neglect. Eight friends helped me repaint the whole place, and, with monies from the Benefit Trust, I spruced it up with new carpets, furnishings and curtains.

It turned out that the husband had been re-housed in a non-disabled flat right next door to me. My ability to mix with all types of people was put to the test with this new neighbour. He was a real rough character who boasted about drinking a bottle of rum and fifteen pints of beer a day. Because of his wife's disability, he knew how difficult everyday life was for me and I knew he wouldn't harm me. Mixed in with the unpleasant side to his nature was kindness. A spirit of willingness to assist those who, in his opinion, had been given an even tougher life than his own. He even helped me to move big pieces of furniture when Duncan wasn't around. The biggest problem was his two Alsatians who he'd leave alone for hours on end.

Certainly in comparison to my previous life my existence was tough. But I knew that my personality hadn't been diminished by what had happened. In fact it had been built upon. My previous zest for life had, in a way, been heightened. I began to laugh more and to speak my mind, something that I'd probably not done with such measure previously for fear that I wasn't going to be liked by people. Now, I knew people liked, if not loved, me. I'd received a living obituary in hospital, something that I see now is a privilege to receive. How many people would wish to attend their own funeral? To see who turns up, to see what is said?

My new, sunny criminal friend was eventually sent to prison for attempted burglary on another neighbour's flat. Then, while he was inside his girlfriend set up a knocking shop in his flat, under the cloak of a hairdressing salon called *Cut and Run*! "Clients" were asked to wait outside while she dealt with her "guest" in the flat. I took this all in my wobbly stride. Living next door to a prostitution racket was at least a step up from my old Rapunzel tower.

Max was phoning regularly. When he was next over in London we met for lunch at a restaurant overlooking Wandsworth Common. It wasn't a very happy occasion. We'd had such a relaxed, physical ease with each other before but now here I was in a different body and I felt awkward. I think, too, that that lunch was the moment where I started to feel great distress at what could have been. At what should have happened in my life. If he *had* left his wife, not that I ever asked that he did, and all that, so I had some resentment in me. I remember quietly looking at him as he talked, thinking, Max, this wouldn't have happened to me if you'd taken me onto a different path. The whole terrible what ifs got to me in a big way. I'd been so deeply in love with him. I would have gone to New York to be with him in a flash. We'd have married and had children. I knew they were damaging, futile thoughts but they wouldn't go away.

At least I could show my weakness with Max and cry my heart out. He showed the deepest compassion and care and, as always, gave me good advice.

'Now is the time to waste darling. Stop. Just stop for a minute.'

On Max's advice, I allowed myself to relax that summer. When not at work I'd lounge around with the soporific spectacle of Wimbledon tennis on the TV and the windows wide open to the glorious June sunshine. I started to feel a little bit OK inside. The lawyers left me mostly alone. Ping, pong, and the summery pong of dog poo from next door's garden wafting in on the breeze. Ping pong poo.

For a while I struggled on with the idea that I'd be able to continue working full-time. I was torn between wanting to do the very best for our clients and the sore reality of my limited mobility. My determination hadn't diminished and my brain was equipped but my body wasn't able to follow on to do the best I wanted to do. The frustrations were significant but people were still reaching out to me, the offers of help and the acts of kindness continued to raise my spirits, often when I was least expecting it.

An extraordinary act of generosity by Richard Price of RPTA/Primetime meant that I became the proud owner of a Golf GTI, equipped with hand controls. One driving lesson later (I had already endured the driving assessment back in February – it was a peculiar process involving carrying out over 40 emergency stops by pushing down on the brake lever with my hand!), and with nerves circulating around my stomach like bees buzzing around flowers, I found myself one day driving on my own to the office.

I began to cry, heaving sobs that threatened to blind me with the tears produced. But they were tears of pride and a little joy. As I operated the push/brake/pull up/accelerator lever around the roads to the office, I realised that this was the first time I'd been on my own and moving in ten months. I felt a temporary surge of freedom in my veins.

Nightmares still made up a considerable portion of my night-time brain activity. The recurring dream of me waving at my old self on the old-fashioned train had been joined by me being forced onto a train. Sometimes the train became a washing machine in a launderette. I would jolt awake, my back wet with perspiration, an ache in my heart and tears on my face. One night the launderette variation was followed by a dream even more terrible about a spooky psychiatrist who wore black and probed his fingers into my brain. This took on additional emphasis the following morning for I was due to receive the first visit from the railway expert, Stanley Hall, and a psychiatrist who was working on an assessment of my mental health for the court case.

The writ had now been served. The trial would be split into two separate parts. The first case for litigation against BR, the second to assess the amount of damages owed – IF the first case was won This meant that when it was over it wouldn't be over at all. Unless I lost.

The psychiatrist asked the necessary questions – focusing on family background and then moving on to the accident itself. On a hot sunny day I was, from head to false foot, wearing black. I had answered his questions comprehensively enough but my head was still slightly in that twilight state when your dream world seems more "real" than the real world. He commented about my choice of clothing and then, to my astonishment, asked, 'Did you have bad dreams last night? And did you dream of a psychiatrist?'

I was impressed and told him so. 'What a dreadful job you have,' I declared with the first smile on my face that day. 'For your clients to experience anxiety nightmares about you before they've even met you.'

CHAPTER THIRTY

Resurrection

Towards the end of that summer my confidence was beginning to feel genuinely restored. I'd been to hell on earth and stared death in the face and survived. And, although few of those around me had been on a similar type of journey, they weren't averse to trying to understand what I'd been through and what I was to continue to go through.

This was to be the beginning of a different type of journey – and one that has taken me years to achieve. To surround myself with the type of people that continue to make me feel good about life. Who open up my mind to the possibilities in living, rather than dwelling upon the impossibilities, the doors now closed. I also felt that I still had one foot – albeit a false one – stuck in the door of relationships, refusing to let that particular door slam completely. One dear friend, Beverly, who'd hired me for the *Brookside* job, was shocked when she'd heard what had happened but not at all fazed. 'You will meet someone very soon,' she said. 'You have an obvious vulnerability now Di, and believe me when I say that some men find that very attractive. Especially in someone who is so strong in other areas of her life.' Not that I was looking. I was too busy getting on with my new life.

These thoughts were only just developing – and again in my subconscious – when Helen and I set off for the wedding of one of her best friends in Yorkshire. She was to be bridesmaid. Her boyfriend Jonny was to be my official "escort" for the occasion, for I still needed assistance on unknown territory.

I was feeling cranky – the push pull strain on my arm as I accelerated and braked around countrified roads on the way to Halifax was sending signals to my brain which emerged from my mouth in the form of twisted petty thoughts rather than the normal expressions of pain.

'I don't want to go to this frigging wedding anyway,' I spat in Helen's general direction. 'It'll be a load of people staring at me as usual, oh look that's *her*. The train. You know. Poor *thing*. Still...' (I repeated a phrase that had crushed my weary heart in Cannes back in April by some insensitive soul) '...it's a good thing she's got such a beautiful sister. At least *she'll* probably have children and she'll be able to be an auntie'.

Helen was silent, fuming at my bitter words. We'd had a bit of a spat already about my going to this wedding. It had ended the previous night with Helen yelling, 'Right, don't bloody well come then.'

The name David suddenly flashed through my brain. Still, I went on. 'Oh, and at these big do's there's bound to be a few criers. You know, the sobbing on MY shoulder. Making me feel like shit.' The name "David" flashed again, and I literally shook my head. 'That's funny,' I said out loud. My voice had softened and Helen's eyes turned to stare at the side of my face as I concentrated on the road ahead. 'What?' she asked, hardly wanting to know the answer.

'The name David keeps coming to my mind.'

'Hardly surprising   our brother in case you'd forgotten, is called DAVID.'

'No, this is different. Why would I want to think about David at this moment?'

'Perhaps,' she hissed, 'he's getting on your nerves as much as my sister is getting on mine.'

I apologised. I was laying troubled thoughts at the wrong door. My dear sister's who only wanted me to have a good time.

We drove straight to the bride's house where Helen was being corseted into her bridesmaid's gear with the other two attendants and the bride, a picture of heaven in frothy white with her flaxen hair. Helen emerged from being made-up and hair-done and twirled like a ballerina in front of me. She looked exquisite. Jonny and I set off for the pub near the church, the meeting place before the ceremony. I held onto Jonny's arm as we entered the pub, every doorstep, lintel, different textured floor capable of bringing me to an un-stoppable fall. As I sipped my drink I looked out of the tiny window to see three DJ-suited men leap off an old-fashioned carriage festooned with wedding ribbon and flowers. I nudged the girl sat next to me. 'Talent approaching. And only one getting hitched hopefully.' We grinned and carried on catching up with the people whose lives we had shared at some point.

'Hello. David.'

A well-modulated, quite posh voice rang in my ear and a secure handshake followed the words. I smiled at the speaker and my thoughts read "um, interesting". He was very handsome, his looks accentuated by his black morning suit. But it was his energy that struck me most. We fell into a conversation that was interrupted almost immediately by the call from the Best Man to get to the church.

After the ceremony Jonny and I drove to the reception. The July sun was glorious, lighting up the surrounding Yorkshire dale scenery and creating an additional warmth to the already happy wedding party. David appeared as if from nowhere with a bottle of champagne in his hand, and he sort of hung around. A lot. Jonny had sunk a few pints in the pub and now began on the champagne in earnest. His bridesmaid girlfriend, my sister, was coming in for much attention. And because it was mainly old boyfriends from her university days, it was, in Jonny's opinion, unwarranted attention which he felt the need to do something about. So he, my now quite tipsy escort, my guiding arm over tricky territory, suddenly disappeared to dance attendance on Helen, whose face was in permanent smile, head thrown back in flirty laughter at the concerted attention she was receiving.

This left David and I to talk and to talk. He continually topped up my drink. I sat on a stone wall and he joined me. We spoke of work – his city business was 'pretty boring really – at best it's a type of industrial espionage.' Doesn't sound boring to me, I thought. In fact it seemed quite fascinating. We shared journalism as a past career and I knew of one of the journals he'd been working on. Suddenly, for time did seem to "fly", we were all asked to be part of a large photo group and then to walk to the building for the wedding breakfast.

Without asking, and with a lovely smile, David held his arm out, gently took one of the sticks and he and I were walking onto the grass with a crowd of others for the photo. In those short minutes we shared what were to become precious words that began to ignite the chemistry that bounced between us. That started to wrap my own battered being into a state of being in love. He asked me what sport did I like to do. I answered quickly, although in surprise, for no-one in the previous year had asked me such a thing. As if it were an impossibility and not under consideration.

'Swimming,' I replied, '– in privacy. And walking is good exercise although of course not very comfortable.'

I knew that he knew about my accident but what surprised me most was that he showed no prurient interest at all. His personality seemed to indicate, as only very close friends could, 'It's happened. Now what are the possibilities in your world?' He gave me the impression that there were many.

'What about golf?' he asked. He began to swing the stick by his side. I looked puzzled. 'It's only a walk in the countryside with a couple of sticks,' he continued.

He held my hand as the photos were taken. It felt warm, comfortable. I leaned slightly against his body. A momentary picture came to my mind of the two of us as a couple. A large, pinch-faced woman made a catty comment about him not keeping his hands to himself. I asked him to explain her attitude as we broke away from the grouping and made our way into the barn style room for the meal.

'My girlfriend's friend,' he muttered. 'Well, sort of my girlfriend. I've moved out. She's one of the other bridesmaids.'

Jonny walked up, his feet slightly behind the rest of his body, as if he was having to concentrate on the act of walking. Which you do if you're drunk.

'Thanks mate,' he shouted at David, 'I'll take over now.' And he grabbed me for the parade in front of the wedding line up. I supported Jonny down the line, shaking hands and kissing cheeks and speaking of nuptial pleasantries. 'The bride looks stunning.' 'I love that waistcoat,' and all the time hissing in Jonny's ear to behave. My drunken escort disappeared again as I approached my seat. I had seen, on the table plan after the line-up, that I had been placed opposite Jonny and next to Nikki, who I knew. And Paul, one of Helen's chaps from university days. Just as I was deciding how Jonny was going to react in front of Paul, David appeared again.

'It seems that fate is throwing us together,' he said. I looked down and sure enough there was his nameplate next to me. A little bride's magic had been woven into the arrangements. Someone had ordered the change of seating plan due to Jonny's over zealous protection of his girlfriend.

David and I talked throughout the meal about our complicated and emotional lives.

'You think yours is tricky,' I said. 'I still live with my ex-fiancee!'

We also giggled about astrology, money (both agreeing that money can bring a certain freedom, if not happiness), other hobbies, and music. Both, again, agreeing when it came to opera that it tended to be rather large people stuffed into overblown costumes stringing out simple phrases with too much noise. We kept the conversation pretty much to ourselves. If it was snatched away by someone else, I soon wrestled it back. I was at my wittiest, and could feel colour in my cheeks.

'Do you know Mahler's 2nd Symphony – *Resurrection*?' He asked, his arms slightly aloft as if he were about to begin conducting. I shook my head.

'It's the most magnificent piece of music in the world. I follow orchestras around who play it.'

My heart had clenched when he used the word Resurrection. It seemed too fitting. A further indicator that we seemed to be speaking in the language code of people who have known each other for a very long time.

After the meal he went to the bar. In a flash Helen appeared beside me. She looked slightly dishevelled, her hair had come down and lay in thick locks framing her excited face.

'What's going on?' she hissed.

'What do you mean?' I said, staring at her with as much post-argument nonchalance that I could muster.

'I've just been told that David thinks you're one of the most beautiful women he's ever met! And his so-called girlfriend isn't very happy about it!'

'Did she suggest the new table arrangement?' I asked.

'Yes, I suppose she did,' Helen nodded. She'd caught my drift.

'Thinking that her straying boyfriend wouldn't be interested in me?'

She grinned. 'But he is, isn't he Di? And he's bloody loaded!'

I said nothing but watched David who was now propping up the bar, speaking to no-one, his eyes drinking in the surrounding party, and resting slightly when he caught my gaze.

The rest of the evening was spent talking to everyone else, intensely aware that I was particularly animated, especially when sharing the occasional words with David, who, by choice, spoke to few others.

It was time to leave and he appeared to help me up from my chair. 'Could I have your address and phone number? I'd very much like to send you that piece of music I told you about.'

We scrabbled for pen and paper, and it seemed rude not to ask – so I took his. He kissed me goodbye three times. Twice on the cheeks and then once quickly on the mouth.

I was too tired to drive. I sat in the back of the car, hugging this music secret to myself, checking and rechecking that his address and phone number were still in my pocket. 'Beautiful writing,' I mused to myself as Helen and Jonny grilled me.

'He seems a very nice chap,' is all I would say. Although I recognised a change in my body chemistry, the thrill in the stomach, the tap at the heart, whenever they mentioned his name. The darkness of the world outside the car suddenly seemed to be pregnant with possibility. I opened the window and breathed in sweet hot air from the trees' and plants' ozone. My soul began to smile.

Daylight brought no doubt that he would get in touch. The only issue in my mind was when. And then, a stabbing insecurity would call to question just what was the big deal? He said he'd send a piece of music – hardly a first hot and heavy date is it? I deliberated. He probably wants to be "friends" another head voice would pipe up. I vowed to just plough on with work, to be cool, to be cool. To be cool.

CHAPTER THIRTY-ONE

Balthazar's Feast

The CD from my handsome Mahler-groupie came a few days later with a note – quite formal but still with that hint of possibility.

My cool exterior was obliterated as I conducted my way around the Tooting flat, classical music throbbing through the walls. The strains of Mahler filled half the street, never mind the flat, so high was the volume. I didn't care one jot. I wheeled and then stood, conducting furiously into a large mirror, eyes and hair alight with energy, looking and feeling ecstatic. I read sleeve notes on the CD and gloried in the majesty of them.

The Symphony No. 2 by Gustav Mahler, known as the *Resurrection Symphony*, was written between 1888 and 1894, and first performed in 1895. Apart from the Eighth Symphony, this symphony was Mahler's most popular and successful work during his lifetime. It is his first major work that would eventually mark his lifelong view of the beauty of afterlife and resurrection. In this large work, the composer further developed the creativity of "sound of the distance" and creating a "world of its own", aspects already seen in his First Symphony.

I read David's note over and over again. He was off on a fishing trip, so it was couple of weeks before I could phone to thank him. His voice was soft and husky as he described the fishing. Poetic phrases about Scottish lochs, bluebells and creaking boats just seemed to trip off his tongue. (He's literary as well, my brain registered in a hopeful surge.) He suggested a drink the following week. Which became dinner.

Our first date was at The Blue Elephant, a Thai restaurant as famed for its plant-life as its food, in the Fulham Road, a fashionable part of west London. We sat at a table set amidst a romantic, jungle-like profusion of palm trees, orchids and greenery. Not that we noticed much about our surroundings. Even the food took fourth place on the menu of activities that night. First came conversation – all five flowing hours of it. The ease with which we talked was a clear indicator to me that it could develop into something more. The waitress must have approached our table for our order at least five times, and each time we would respond, 'Sorry, just ten more minutes!' Drink took a staggering second place. Topics of conversation held their own at third place – loss of virginity, books, travel. Food came last. Laughter ran like water throughout the meal and when he finally poured me into a black cab at gone midnight, I could literally feel the chemistry sparking between us. Before we parted I asked him to a concert at the Royal Albert Hall. A friend was singing. I forced the "casual" into my voice, thinking desperately, 'please, please, please don't say no.'

He didn't say no but phoned a few days later sounding upset. He said he didn't think he could make it. Emotional journalism took over my voice as I delved into the why with a combination of questions and silence. He finally conceded that the relationship with his girlfriend, while over from his point of view, was still causing problems. She couldn't let go. (And his male ego wouldn't let him go, I surmised.) The words "be cool" sang their mantra in my head. I suggested that he didn't make a final decision on the concert. Perhaps you need a bit of time on your own? There was still ten days to go. Ten days for me to change his mind.

I threw myself into my work, apart from my family and friends, virtually the only constant event in my life which predated the accident and an extremely significant feature of my rehabilitation. I had to persevere in this work despite the adverse circumstances. There were many tensions. I was determined to carry on but the nature of the business I was in couldn't, in some ways, have been much worse.

Sarah and I had met when I was working on *TV World* magazine as Deputy Editor and she was Head of Advertising. Headhunted onto two other magazines, into senior positions, I'd developed a growing Little Black Book of contacts and spotted the opportunity, the classic gap in the market, for a PR company geared to the world TV markets. I could see Sarah was a brilliant administrator so I approached her and suggested starting the business. In short, I had been the driving force behind the company.

Unfortunately the production and programming side of the broadcasting industry is a glamorous one and didn't accept disability easily. You have to be fast, attractive and mobile to succeed. As a whole, people related to me as a disabled person, rather than a person who happens to have a disability.

Getting the coal from the face, getting the coverage for the programmes in the mainstream press, had been my main role. Now it was Sarah's. She was shy and lacking in confidence rather than the "cold" that people sometimes thought. She simply wasn't as at ease in situations in the same way that I was. And, although a certain amount of PR work could be done then by phone and fax without leaving a desk, clients frequently demanded our physical presence. Not only to make introductions, generally "host" or "moderate" media meetings and interviews but also to perform what is known in the business as a "hand holding job". Location filming was out for me. It's fast, furious, and often in the middle of fields in obscure places. Time was always at a premium, measured in minutes and seconds. I had no choice but to stay back in the office and hand over most of the hand holding side to Sarah. I'd been a natural in this role, but, being less outgoing and much more of a reactive than a proactive, Sarah wasn't.

I succeeded in getting David to the concert with a little help from some literary "friends". Notably John Fowles, brilliant author of *The Magus* which I packaged up with a pleasant note and delivered to his door a few days after our phone conversation. He returned the favour with Isabel Allende's *Eva Luna* and a postcard saying that he felt *The Magus* was one of the most profound books he'd ever read. I devoured Allende in one sitting that weekend and sent him a fax. A flurry of faxes ensued – with cartoons drawn by David and witty words scribbled by me.

He mentioned that he was trying to arrange some "private swimming". I was intrigued. I was now thinking about him most of the time, a sure sign that you're a goner on the love stakes. The dreamy distraction that comes over you as you're talking to friends. The slight judder in your body when the phone rings. Or, in my particular case, whenever the fax bell trilled its signal that a message was on its way.

With other friends I had hired a box for the concert at the Royal Albert Hall. We drank champagne and David and I held hands and laughed at my stomach rumbling.

'What will stop that noisy stomach of yours?' whispered David.

'Nuts – have you got any?' I quietly giggled back, wondering whether it was hunger or actually a passionate lust that was causing the tummy wobbles. 'Oh, and some chocolate cake.'

The music was magnificent – *Balthazar's Feast* by Sibelius, complete with a soaring finale that Mahler would have been proud of.

The next day a large package was delivered to the excited offices of MediaVision. Sarah hopped from foot to foot with glee, delighted at my renewed vigour and continuous laughing. It was a chocolate cake and about twenty packets of nuts. With it came a mysterious note that said I should meet him with my swimming costume at the RAC Club, a private gentleman's club, in Piccadilly, central London.

I took Helen along and we met David in the very grand reception area, full of tapestries, wood panels and broad, sweeping staircases. He introduced me to the manager who explained that the swimming pool had been freed up for me to swim in privacy for the next hour. Rather coyly, I left David sitting in a large armchair while Helen and I made our way down to the pool. We got changed behind the marble columns that were planted around the edge of the beautiful floodlit pool. Again, it was a joy to be in soothing water, feeling the effects of exercise on my body. When I returned upstairs David had fallen fast asleep in the chair.

I felt rather silly – not asking if he would have liked to have joined me. I just felt that the physical was a little behind on the emotional and mental leaps and bounds of our friendship. However, I asked him the next time because, by then, we had kissed. In fact we had shared a whole day – clay pigeon shooting in the morning; a play at Regent's Park Open Air Theatre in the afternoon, and then dinner at La Famiglia, a beautiful Italian restaurant, in the evening. We managed to polish off not one but three bottles of champagne. He walked more badly than I towards the cab that night, and then we staggered into his Knightsbridge flat to drink coffee, conduct loud music and attempted to sober up. We stayed up all night talking, snogging and holding hands and when it rained we stood outside on the roof terrace, clasping each other, letting it pelt our faces, mouths wide open, laughing and drinking the water from the heavens.

CHAPTER THIRTY-TWO

I Could Have Danced All Night

We returned to the RAC the following week and this time David came into the pool with me. I felt only a slight edge of embarrassment which he banished completely as he took me in his arms and we danced in the gleaming turquoise water. 'You are my beautiful mermaid,' he said as we danced around and around singing *I Could Have Danced All Night* from *My Fair Lady*. Held in his powerful arms, my sarong and hair fanned out in the water as he spun me around, my body felt a freedom long forgotten and my soul, at last, began to dance again.

With caution.

The chemistry between us couldn't be doubted but he'd obviously been a player in his not too distant past. On top of which his ex was still hovering on the peripheries making life difficult for both of us. This included her sending David the full list of over one hundred women who worked with her on a national newspaper, with their corresponding direct line phone nos and the message: "You could have had any one of these women, they all have legs".

David had taken his time about delivering this latest bitter diatribe from his ex, and with good reason – it was as if I was so very not good enough. Even for him, who had treated his ex-girlfriend very badly, yet here she was, in her sadness, trying to make me feel like I was an untouchable. I was open to letting him know how keen I was on him but held back on talking about the dreaded "future". I simply wouldn't have been able to survive having my heart broken again. Instead, we continued seeing each other on a long, wonderful drawn-out courtship. We'd frequently sit up until dawn just talking. The ball, I knew, was in my court. I'd have to say when I was ready for the next, the physical, stage.

David put no pressure on me, he couldn't have been more empathetic. He'd been in the army and had witnessed first hand the terrible injuries the tools of war can produce. He'd had a parachute accident himself and still suffered from a bad back. In the end it all happened very naturally, just like our first meeting at the wedding. I was going to Cannes for the October MIPCOM and invited David to come with me.

It was a wonderful time and I allowed myself full acceptance. I was in love. We became a couple and, over dinner beneath the stars on the Cannes Croisette, with the sea lapping gently in the background, we felt comfortable enough with each other to analyse together what had first attracted us to each other.

Why was I falling in love with David? How could I not? He had parts in him of every man I had loved. The whole package. My fears that I'd have to compromise in my love life and accept whoever came forward had taken a surprise twist. I'd landed a catch. Intelligent, funny, cultured, a little bit odd with his crazy Mahler twist, good-looking, empathetic and kind. Money had never been important to me but obviously the fact that he was comfortably off was a bonus. We could afford to go out to restaurants, to travel and to stay in hotels which could cater to my needs.

Why did David fall in love with me? He'd been in a relationship for two years when we met at the wedding. His girlfriend had been one of the bridesmaids. It hadn't been going well and he had been fooling around, sleeping around and driving fast cars. At the point we met he'd reached a stage where he knew his life was very unsatisfactory emotionally. After the initial pull of my looks (he said he "wasn't a leg man anyway!"), it was my aura of strength that first attracted him. After we'd parted all he knew was that he wanted to see me again. Our first date was very different from any other he'd been on. Unlike most of his first dates, a potential relationship, let alone sex, wasn't on his mind. Yet he felt more nervous than usual. So something was going on. Our minds met and he found for the first time that he didn't want to rush anything.

My "sexlessness" fears proved, but for all the right reasons rather than the wrong ones.

CHAPTER THIRTY-THREE

Get Here

It started going pear-shaped soon after our return from Cannes. The strain on David was beginning to show. I was certain that the worry of me, of living with my damaged life, not to mention the building stress of the legal fight, had got to him.

Hoping more time together abroad would ease the pressures, I readily agreed to accompany him on a business trip to Tokyo and New York. He was working of course, but his manner changed quite dramatically. It all came to a head when he left our room in our New York skyscraper hotel one day, leaving me in the bath, with the words "I need to go back to my ex". With super-human effort, I heaved myself out of that deep bath and bottomed along the cold tiles to reach my wheelchair, to put my "legs" on.

I called Max who delayed the first day of his new job to come to "rescue" me. He helped me reschedule my return flight. I left New York. David would return to an empty hotel room with a bath-tub full of cold water. After such powerful action, Max was certain that David would come back for me. 'Give him 3 weeks,' were his parting words. 'He will be begging to have you back.'

Flying on my own was a courageous thing to do, even by my standards. But I felt strongly that I should get out of David's way and give him time alone without me to think. Did he really want to take me on? And did I really want to be with someone capable of such behaviour?

Back in London he kept on sending me notes. He kept phoning. He wrote long letters. I could sense the confusion in his words. He wanted to stay in touch.

Stay in touch? Not enough! I didn't respond but prayed hard he'd return to the fold.

A skin graft on one of my legs was preventing me from having a new prosthetic. This added to the pain and frustrations but I threw myself into work and tried hard not to think about him. Not too successfully. I drove Sarah at work, and Duncan at home, crazy, my behaviour reverting to that of a lovelorn teenager.

Finally, six weeks later, after I judged that a suitable amount of distance had been created, and he'd shown no signs of giving up, I agreed to meet. He knew how horrible he'd been to me in New York and pleaded for me to take him back.

Our first reunion date since parting was dramatic. David arranged for his pilot friend to fly us to Le Touquet for a long, champagne-fuelled lunch. When we kissed at the end of day, he said: 'I never want to let you go again. Ever.'

After a wonderful Christmas I joined David skiing in Switzerland and we celebrated the New Year in together. We were now fully committed to each other. I sometimes stayed with David in Knightsbridge but more often he'd stay with me in the Tooting flat, equipped for my needs.

'I think it's time I moved out,' said Duncan one morning.

'You don't have to do that, Dunky,' I replied.

'I think I do. You're going to marry this man aren't you?'

I didn't want to be too confident about that but Duncan, who had a steady girlfriend by then, moved out soon afterwards.

David and I were happy in our love but there was a lot of strain. I had the legalities to deal with and David had his own work problems in the banking world.

My continuing visits to the hospital were one thing, but the pressures that the lead-up to the trial caused were immense and came in many forms. From small irritations, like my own solicitors arranging a trial date at a time when my business partner would be away on holiday, to challenging face to face interrogations. Eventually the trial date was settled for three days in February and Steve brought Simon Wakefield QC, and his Junior Counsel to the flat to interview me.

Steve hadn't given me any warning that there would be this rigorous court-like close questioning from my own side. This came as a great shock and fuelled the worry of it all.

'Why did I rush? Why did I board a moving train? Why did I ignore the guard?'

'I didn't! I didn't I DIDN'T!'

'Was your Walkman too loud?'

'No.'

'So you *were* wearing a Walkman?'

'Yes BUT IT WASN'T ON – the Walkman obviously wasn't playing on the tracks – it's in Saville's, the BR Area Manager's, report.'

'That testimony won't be used, Diana, but they'll still suggest that you were listening to it and thus negligent.'

'I WASN'T LISTENING TO IT!'

'Even though Saville lied they'll STILL USE IT.'

'HOW CAN THEY!'

'To sow the seeds of doubt in the judge's mind.'

Steve said we could subpoena Mr Saville if we needed to. A subpoena is a legal order commanding the person or organisation named in the subpoena to give sworn testimony at a specified time.

QC Wakefield then warned that they'll try and discredit me in every way they can think of. They had already queried my use of contact lenses. 'We believe her vision was impeded.' I had to point out, in a written statement, that contact lenses actually improve vision – including peripheral.

My original statement stated that a woman got on the train in front of me. I thought, so I confirmed, because the door was open. But she hadn't come forward. Was I sure?

I repeated that the door was ajar when I tried to board, that's why I wasn't expecting the train to move.

We moved on to witnesses. There are only two, they say, it's me against the guard. He's an employee of seven years with a good service record and I'm the jet setting Champagne Charlotte with her own company living with her ex. Who is the judge going to believe?

My uneasiness hit a new low. As the date approached, Steve kept assuring me that we had got a case. But he kept me informed of developments in a way I didn't much care for, like he was treating it as a game. I reached such a state of paranoia I began to wonder about the whole legal system and then, increasingly, about my own side. I wasn't at all convinced that my own side really understood what had happened on the day of the accident. Although the nightmares continue to haunt, I wasn't even sure myself now that my memory had faded. I couldn't believe that I should be made to feel so persecuted when I have been so tragically injured.

At the end of one of our many, many long phone calls, where I had sobbingly announced, 'but I know what I say is the truth, Steve.' He declared, with sincerity:

'Sometimes Di, the truth is not enough.'

In the end British Rail declared five witnesses. The guard, the driver, the ticket collector, the area manager and myself. The good news was that they didn't have an expert. This indicated that they, arrogantly, weren't expecting a fight. Plus we'd nabbed the top man, Stan Hall, first. The crucial braking distances we had were Stan's figures, not official figures, but he was British Rail's safety man for a decade. We were therefore not going to ask for official figures as the whole case would probably end up resting on this evidence.

I was still using work to distract myself from my terrible situation. On the night before the court case I worked until 11pm and was rewarded with a very big client. Dad phoned asking me to repeat over and over again: The train was not moving. 'That, he said, 'is all you need to remember.'

In the taxi on the way to Court I let my solicitor Simon Wakefield's words of reassurance run over and over again in my mind. British Rail are a national company with a declining safety record, slashing running costs to make themselves profitable as they prepare for privatisation. They've lied and bullied a woman who has lost both her legs.

I was nervous, beyond measure. Adrenalin flooded my entire body, even breathing seemed difficult. But I wanted to tell these bullies the truth. That's if I could get into the courtroom.

The High Courts, built in the 1870s, are a warren of stone corridors, steeped in history and riddled with steps. Still unable to walk more than 20 feet (6 metres) without feeling severe pain and dizziness, especially with the nerve-jangling stress coursing through me as I prepared for the "fight", I needed to use the wheelchair. Fortunately we had given ourselves a lot of time to find the courtroom. It took my three "helpers" – David, sister Helen and her partner, Jonny – and I over half an hour to eventually locate the room via two horrible dark, clanking "service" lifts, wheeling and walking. Oh, the irony.

The hum and bustle of the courtroom preparing for trial stilled for a moment as we entered. Nobody looked our way but the hush told us loud and clear that they had all noted our arrival. I looked around – the lawyers in their robes and wigs, the countless clerks only there for the 9-5 before going back to their real lives; the little corner of informal humanity in the public gallery. It looked more like a film set and didn't seem real at all. An

161

impression that I relayed to my three musketeers. It became even harder to believe or fully comprehend what was happening.

'All rise,' said a voice. The judge entered and everybody except me stood up, blocking my view. One of those moments where, if I hadn't been so scared, I wouldn't have known whether to laugh or cry.

I glared angrily at the backs of everybody's bottoms now at face-level. I didn't feel at all prepared. I didn't feel like I'd been given enough advice on how to get through it. I looked down at my lap. My doubts had been growing to such an extent I had started to really wonder if my own side were really on my side. The "game" element had intensified. It sometimes felt like they were more determined to win a case for the usual brownie points rather than seeing justice for me.

Everybody sat down and moments later I heard my name being called. I wheeled myself into the witness box to be cross-examined by BR's tough, flamboyant QC.

'Now, Miss Hill, when you look back to that day, does it all seem like, well, like a film?'

My low level paranoia ratcheted up – had they been listening in to my conversations? I took my time in answering, my calm delivery belying my scrambling brain.

'Um, do you mean like a horror movie?'

A stifled snigger broke out – from the direction of the press bench.

The detail I had to go into was frightening. So many tiny day-to-day things that you never, ever expect to be examined on, grow and grow into significance.

We started off with my ticket. I had a ticket but didn't show it to Mr Levi the ticket barrier man because I passed him so often – this had been the fourth time just on that day. He knew I had a ticket. Simple day to day logic. But before the case could even go ahead they needed proof that I'd been travelling with a valid ticket which had to be confirmed in court. I had actually destroyed my weekly ticket, but, thankfully, could show them the Barclaycard statement. (If I hadn't had proof of payment I would not have been able to take them to court.)

Keeping emotion at bay as much as I could, I gave a detailed explanation of how I'd gone down the stairs, proceeding one at a time.

'I wasn't relaxed, exactly, but you can't hurry that quickly. I went down as fast as I reasonably could.

'When I got to the foot of the stairs the train was stationary. I heard some doors slamming. I heard no signal that the train was about to leave.

The door was ajar. I went up to the train and opened it with my left hand. I stepped onto the train, onto the running board. It was still stationary. I remember seeing all the passengers' doors, but I don't know the exact whereabouts of my door on the train in relation to the others. I went to raise my other leg up to get into the train and the train moved off.'

We moved on to on the guard's warning which I hadn't heard.

'My Walkman wasn't switched on. If he'd shouted "stand away" I would have heard it. Others would have heard it.'

I was pulled up. That wasn't the point here, other witnesses would be called to confirm my memory of this non-event event.

'With a jolt, the train started to move. I tried to keep my balance but my heavy bag seemed to be pulling me off. It pulled me back round to the right. It was the weight of the bag, not that it was caught on anything. I couldn't keep my balance on the running board and fell.' I paused for a moment, picking up on the chilled silence all around me, before forcing myself to continue, keeping my tone as steady and as level as I could. Letting the truth come out as it happened. 'I was wedged between the moving train and the platform, with my stomach to the platform and my back to the train. I was still upright. The door had seemed to move in an opening direction. I don't remember which bit of it I had hold of. But now I wasn't holding onto anything. I automatically put my arm up and my head forward because I was aware that the train was still moving. I was shocked but it was in my mind that I must scream because the train didn't seem to be stopping.'

My voice finally gave out. The worst thing was the complete lack of response. Not a flicker of empathy, not a grain of humanity, crossed that man's face. Instead he took my sorrow as a point for his team's side and launched into a follow-up of quickfire close questioning to try and catch me out. To prove that I was lying about whether the train had been moving or not.

Why did I rush?

Had I ignored the guard's warning?

Did I think I could get on the train as it had only just started?

'I didn't try to get on a moving train and the guard didn't shout.'

I concentrated on keeping my cool, answering him one question at a time.

'What happened next?'

'Instead of slowing down and stopping, the train pushed me further up against the platform. It was painful. My chest felt the pain. I screamed once and when the pain got bad I screamed relentlessly. Until then I thought that obviously the train would be stopping. But the train didn't stop....' I paused to collect myself.

'I fell.'

Every person in the room seemed to draw in their breath as one. The silence was deafening, like all the air had been sucked into a vacuum.

'I received two big electric shocks to the left leg,' I continued. 'I wasn't sure if my body was then still in the same position in relation to the platform. I seemed to be on the track. How did I get there? I scrabbled with my hands, struggling to get to the top of the platform. I was screaming not for help now but because of the pain. The unbearable pain. Then I looked down and saw....'

I had to stop for a moment. I didn't cry but struggled to keep my composure.

'....that my right leg was nearly not part of my body.'

There followed a series of quickfire questions that I should never have been asked to endure.

'I'm not sure if I had my fingers on the platform or if I was trying to reach it. I couldn't really see behind me but I know that the wheel was on top of my left leg. I was wholly down on the train level. Where was my head? My head was towards the platform. My left leg was under the train. I was face down. No, I don't know when the Walkman got separated. Yes, my bag was with me when the train stopped.'

Finally, it was over.

I kept my head down as I was wheeled out of the witness box. I couldn't possibly have looked at anybody in the eye. All I could think was why? *How* had my life got to this?

The first of our witnesses to be called by our own prosecuting QC was Debbie. She'd been sitting in the fourth carriage of the train, very close to the accident, reading the paper at the time. Her window was open half way down. She didn't hear a shout or a whistle blow before the train moved.

She didn't hear the guard shout "stand away" or anything like that. She heard me screaming. Responding to the crucial question – before or after the train moved? – she remembered the train pulling off with a jolt and she didn't hear anything. Then the train started to move and *as the train started to move* she heard screaming. She heard continual screaming while the train was moving. When the train stopped it juddered violently. She couldn't say if the screaming went on. Everyone was getting off the train, so it was noisy. She saw the black man walking down by the platform shaking his head and four children watching... At this point Our QC emphasised the lost potential of many witnesses.

Then came Maggie, my angel, the woman whose group I'd rushed past at the ticket barrier.

Maggie was sure that the train hadn't been moving when I went past them at the ticket barrier because she remembers hearing the train start to pull away as she walked over the footbridge, having already gone past me at the ticket barrier. They heard the screaming and they all went back through the barrier and down to that platform. She described the arrival of the ambulance crew and the police. She didn't see a Walkman or headphones. Her first awareness of the BR staff was when they were trying to coordinate their efforts to move the train off me.

Kate Lowe heard just one scream first, then a pause and then continuous screaming. Kate's husband, John Lowe confirmed that he hadn't heard "stand away" or a whistle.

'I asked the ticket collector if he'd called the ambulance and was surprised that he hadn't. I rushed to the main ticket office and the lady called the emergency services immediately. Whilst I waited for the ambulance, she went down to the platform, returning with a comment something like "silly girl, getting on a moving train..." I assumed she'd spoken to guard or driver.'

At that point came a thought that hadn't occurred to me, or anybody else, before that moment. Hadn't the guard and the driver both said they'd called the emergency services already? Was THAT why the BR Policewoman arrived BEFORE the ambulance? Wasn't this yet another layer of cover-up by these incompetents that should have been examined by my own side? Too late now...

Anger surged through me. I had to restrain myself from shouting out in such a way that nobody would ever forget it – THE TRAIN WASN'T MOVING.

John Lowe confirmed there had been about 20 people milling about platform. My QC stopped him there to again ram the point home that there had been 20 potential witnesses to the accident that BR hadn't thought to take details of.

'I heard a BR official asking the guard and driver what had happened. It sounded like a pretty superficial account to me. I heard the guard saying, "I saw her go under and I pulled the cord". I can't remember the guard saying anything about whether or not the train was moving when she had tried to board. I remember the driver sort of nodding and saying "when that happened I stopped the train".'

Nobody had asked him if he'd seen what had happened, they'd taken his name and address but that was all.

I tensed further as the doctor was called to confirm my injuries.

'Severe laceration, degloving, fracture of the tibia, fibula on the right...'

'*Is that enough?*' I wanted to shout at all the Alice in Wonderland type grotesques in their idiotic costumes. 'Can we go home now? Why am I having to prove this. *Look at me – just listen to this and look.*'

'...her left leg showed degloving of the skin, extended from the distal part of the thigh to the proximal third of the tibia. Comminute fracture of the fibula...'

Paradoxically the electric shocks may have saved my life, cauterising the wound and putting me into state of shock that temporarily numbed the true sensation of the pain I was in.

'She was admitted with both legs still attached, but both damaged well beyond repair. After 48 hours her right stump showed brownish discoloration of the distal part of the flap. This led to a series of corrective surgeries to save the remaining stump and allow it to support eventual prosthesis. The majority of her ribs were broken, but that,' he concluded, 'was the least of her problems.'

CHAPTER THIRTY-FOUR

The End Of Innocence

That evening I discussed the further ramifications of the case with my sister Helen, her husband Jonny and, of course, David. They relayed their thoughts to counsel, who by and large ignored them. The feeling grew that nobody seemed to really understand the case — especially the leading counsel who'd only met me once.

I tried my hardest to cope but it was overwhelming. The stress levels were the highest I'd ever known. One of the lowest points came at me suddenly and without warning when Christopher Johnsons's video of the trains arriving at the platform were shown. It wasn't the sight of the trains, I could bury my face in my hands, but the sounds of them. A Proustian moment which took me straight back to the moment of my fall.

The focus turned to the blind spot beside the stairs. The video evidence showed that the guards' heads sometimes disappeared into their cabins for a vital few seconds, up to 3.5, when they rang the start bell. I reverted to my hospital tactics when the pain of reality became too hard to bear. The usual nightmares, I told myself. It would be morning soon enough.

Instead, the next thing I heard was, 'Call Mr Saville'.

My eyes shot open. With heart racing, I eyeballed the On Call Duty Manager as he went to the stand. A curly feeling of fascination joined the repulsion. Here, then, was the man who'd lied about the Walkman. Here was the man who told everybody I'd boarded a moving train. Here was the man who didn't think it necessary to call an enquiry, to hunt for witnesses.

After he was bleeped at 18.34 he went to the scene and interviewed the guard, the driver, and Mr Levi, the ticket collector. All said I'd boarded a moving train.

He didn't think to question that, no. He didn't take statements from the public, no – there were no witnesses on or near the platform who'd seen the accident. Our QC pointed out John Lowe volunteering his details. How would he have known Mr Lowe hadn't seen the accident if he wasn't asked?

And why was the train allowed to continue on its journey without an enquiry? Because there was no fault with the train! The crew had followed emergency procedure when called upon and the driver said he was fit and able to proceed to Victoria. They couldn't have an enquiry every time someone tries to board a moving train or they'd never run.

When asked about recovering the Walkman from the track he looked uncomfortable, aware of his indiscretion and its evidence having been withdrawn by BR. It was so frustrating to know that his whopper about the Walkman still playing wasn't allowed to be referred to. Again, I had to refrain from shouting it out loud and clear. It didn't seem right, it wasn't right, how could it be fair that the judge didn't know about this?

Mr Levi the ticket collector came next. He said I ran past him. That he shouted to me for my ticket but I kept running. The train was already moving, he said, when I got to the barrier. He was asked to repeat this. That the train had already departed before I even got to the platform.

I was getting increasingly panicky and uncomfortable. I breathed deeply. Next came Mr Higham the driver. I hadn't been able to recall the faces of the guard or the driver – it was the biggest shock of all to see them. I don't know why, but I felt stupid for feeling so surprised to see them there. It had to be some kind of instinctive protection that the brain had put in place, unable to bear the anticipation beforehand.

He'd been a train driver for eleven years.

'The signal was two bells to move. I'd moved about 6 to 7 yards (6 metres) when one bell, the emergency stop signal, was given. I immediately applied the emergency brakes and left the cab to find out the problem. I saw the guard running towards me. He said he'd just seen a woman trying to board the moving train. She'd slipped and gone underneath. I went to the signal box to telephone, isolate the line and call the emergency services.'

There were no further questions and the sickening feeling inside notched up even higher. The Guard, Paul Crookshank, the man who'd ruined my life, was called and I began to shiver uncontrollably.

His suit didn't fit him, his black hair greasy with primal fear. In my mind he was a criminal, he looked like a dressed up football hooligan, with all the aggressive anger removed. He seemed so scared I thought the judge would feel sorry for him.

He spoke. He'd been employed for 7 years… That was enough.

The judge was imperious but had a kindly manner. He was the first to notice how upset I was.

Proceedings were stopped so that I could wheel myself out of court.

David, Helen and Jonny filled me in on his evidence that evening.

No passengers alighted, about 3 passengers boarded the train. When all of the doors were closed, he looked up and down the platform and saw no other passengers wishing to board. He gave the signal to the driver to depart by giving two rings of the bell. The train started to move away and he continued to look out of the brake van as the train was leaving the platform. Ahead of him on the platform were some stairs leading to the footbridge, suddenly he saw me appear on the platform from the stairs. He shouted to me to stand away.

He shouted a warning but I took no notice and I ran towards the train and opened the train door while the train was moving. He then saw me slip down between the train and the platform.

He then gave the emergency stop signal to the driver by giving one ring on the bell. He also applied the emergency brake in his Guards Brake van.

He had, he said, carried out all the necessary emergency procedures.

There were no further questions for the guard from BR's counsel. This, we agreed, was good news but none of us dared to feel even a little more confident. Expectations couldn't come into it. It was all too important.

I returned to the courtroom for the opposing QC's summing up.

'We have heard how common it is for people to attempt to board a moving train. We have established that Miss Hill was rushing for the train, even bumping into people in her haste. We have established that the witnesses presented by the prosecution didn't actually witness the accident, and those that did haven't come forward despite public appeals. We have heard that emergency procedure was dutifully followed and sadly we must conclude that this tragic incident is solely the responsibility of Miss Hill. I will cite Titchener v BRB "volenti non fit inuria", "to the willing, no injury is done".

We've lost.

Even I think I'm guilty.

CHAPTER THIRTY-FIVE

Sue Me, Sue You

This was all about me but it didn't feel like it was about me at all. It felt more like a legal batting game. The evening before what was to be the third and final day I asked my counsel what he felt the outcome would be.

'It depends, Diana, on what the judge has for breakfast.'

It was a casual remark – and certainly wasn't meant unkindly but the throwaway nature of it summed up all my feelings of helplessness. I couldn't convince him on what should be said because I didn't have the hidden language codes used in law.

And so on the third day came our QC Simon Wakefield's chance to cross-examine British Rail's witnesses. I was determined to be there for every second of it.

It was the toughest day of my life.

The discomfort for British Rail started early when Mr Levi, the ticket collector, took to the stand.

'How,' Simon Wakefield enquired, 'did he know the train was moving when I passed him when he couldn't see the train from his ticket collecting box?'

As it could have been the southbound train at Platform 1, he had no credible defence and was swiftly dispatched.

Then came our expert Stan Hall with all the back-up of his precise measurements and calculations. As a former Safety Standards Officer for British Rail and the author of several seminal books on railway accidents, everybody in the Court knew there was no greater expert on the subject. If the train had been moving at that time I simply would never have been able to catch it. The train had travelled, Stan said, for approximately 9 seconds. Stopping where it did suggested that not only was it standing when I alighted, but that the emergency brake wasn't applied as quickly as it should have been.

If the train guard saw me trying to board a moving train, under rule A.1.5.1 the emergency signal should have been given. If it had, I wouldn't have fallen down between the coaches. Stan backed this up by reeling off a whole list of BR safety rules and regulations.

If the train wasn't moving when I opened the door, but started to move when I had my foot on the running board, Stan thought it was possible that the "ready to start" bell signal to the driver had already been given. As soon as he realised I was boarding the train he should have given the "stop" bell signal immediately. The train would have had an open door so it should have been stopped for this reason alone. If the Guard had given the correct emergency response the train would have stopped within a few feet. Instead of shouting "stand away", he should have treated the situation as an emergency from that moment as he saw me boarding the train. Though the guard says he did treat it as an emergency, the train stopped too far down the track to be consistent with that. Either the Guard didn't see the accident or if he did see it, he took emergency action too late.

Then it was the Guard's turn. Helen, David and Jonny were as one, each poised to wheel me out but, with my confidence raised by what had already happened, I was all set for the final truth to come out. This was it now: his word against my own.

Asked about the gap in time between giving the signal and moving, the guard accepted that there was a possibility of not being able to see during those crucial few seconds. He'd never used the emergency brake on a passenger train before.

There followed a picking-apart of his written statement I'm glad I was able to find the strength to witness.

His statement said that he'd suddenly seen a woman on the platform from the stairs, that "the woman" had jumped down the last set of stairs. He agreed that he hadn't see a woman on the stairs but had "presumed it".

As crossing his blind spot from the stairs to the train would take a second, he was asked how long the train had been moving when I suddenly appeared. He couldn't say how long exactly, but estimated 3 seconds.

He couldn't explain why nobody heard his shouted warning. He reiterated that he did shout. Once. By the time he'd shouted I had the door open.

Though, from the witness box, he didn't agree with Stan's calculation that after 3 seconds the train would have been going too quickly for anybody to board, he had changed his statement estimate from "2 or 3 seconds", to "just as the train had started to move", ie 1 to 2 seconds.

He didn't see an open door as an emergency, saying people are always opening doors as the train gets into a station – I thought this shocking.

But that was coming to a stop, not speeding up to leave – didn't he think this was an emergency? In hindsight he agreed it was an emergency.

But not an emergency before I started to open the door. So was the door open when he shouted Stand Away?

No the door was closed.

So why did he shout stand away?

Questioned about how long it took for the emergency to arise, he agreed the timing of 4 or 5 seconds. He was questioned on his estimation of the train stopping distance of 46 feet (14 metres), way short of the actual distance of 122 feet (37 metres).

Did he agree that if he'd acted when he first saw me, the train would have stopped in half the distance and the accident wouldn't have happened? He agreed that if he'd acted faster the train could have stopped in half the distance it actually did.

It was difficult to keep quiet as I sat there watching him. This stranger who had ruined my life. WHY hadn't he acted faster? Again, it felt criminal.

'Do you agree that if you had acted when you first saw Miss Hill, the train would have stopped in half the distance averting this tragic accident? Do you agree that if that person who crossed the platform had been frail, or, for example, a wheelchair user, you would have stopped the train from moving off?'

'I agree that if I had acted faster the train could have stopped in half the distance it actually did.'

'Then why didn't you?'

'I presumed she'd be able to get on.'

'An audible exhalation of breath whirled around the room. Realising his disastrous error, Crookshank looked down at his feet.

'Can you repeat that please,' said our QC quietly. It was pure Perry Mason. I had by now totally stopped breathing. It was for conclusive moments like that, I realised, that people like him were paid so very highly. I wanted to hug all the breath out of him.

'Please repeat that for me,' he said again.

'I thought she'd make it.'

Then he twisted it in, 'So you delayed using the emergency brake?'

'I delayed using the emergency brake, because I thought she'd make it.'

'Did you stop the train because you became alerted to Miss Hill's presence by her scream?'

'I heard no scream until the train stopped. I should have heard her but I didn't. I first heard her scream when I was on the platform.'

'By not acting, you inferred an invitation to board the train.'

'It didn't occur to me that I was giving her the chance to get on.'

'You are in breach of the safety rules and you failed to act in the proper manner to protect yourself.'

'It wasn't because of the breach that I didn't spell it out. I wasn't trying to protect myself.'

'You didn't protect Miss Hill.'

'I could have done more than I did. I accept that in all probability the train would have stopped far sooner and Miss Hill's injuries would have been far less.'

'Was the train even moving?'

'If the train had been standing still, I would have given another ring on the bell.'

'You mean, if you had seen her when she tried to board?'

'As soon as I saw her go down I wished I'd acted earlier.'

'Tell me again, why did you wait for 9 seconds to brake?'

'I don't believe the 9 seconds is right in my heart but I can't argue with it. I can't account for the distance the train travelled.'

'No further questions.'

I glanced at Helen. A tiny, triumphant smile crossed her lips but she couldn't look at me. He'd just admitted his mistake had cost me my legs. None of us could quite believe it.

The judge called the BR QC.

'No questions.'

It was over.

Still not daring to look at each other, we left the courtroom.

I was given the choice of hearing the judge's summing up on the following day or that afternoon. David and I went for a quiet lunch. I stared out of the taxi window, looking everywhere for signs, for hidden codes. On our way back to court I pointed out a statue of Richard the Lionheart.

'At least it wasn't Oliver Cromwell,' we joked nervously together.

We returned to our places in the court room. As our QC Simon Wakefield stood to begin his summing up, the sound of heightened courtroom chatter falling to a dramatic hush put the fear of God into me.

'The case turns on the answers to the following questions of fact. One: Was the train already moving when Miss Hill opened the door? Two: Did Mr Crookshank shout "Stand Away?" Three: Did the driver and the guard bring the train to a halt with the rapidity to be expected if the guard was keeping a proper look out and acted as he should have? 'For the first two questions, there is the evidence of Miss Hill. She is an honest witness, she did not guess answers and admitted when she could not remember. She said that she heard no warning of "Stand Away", she could scarcely be mistaken as she was within 30 feet of the guard compartment.

Miss Crammond, only a coach away with a window open, also heard no warning but she did hear Miss Hill's screaming before the train stopped. Mr and Mrs Lowe and Miss Davis also heard the screams but not a warning shout. Even Mr Levi, the ticket collector did not mention a warning shout, rather by inference that the train was going so fast that the guard would have been well down the platform. A case now abandoned.

So did the driver and guard bring the train to a halt, with the speed of an emergency action that is to be expected if the guard had been keeping a proper look out? The answer lends support to Miss Hill's case that the train was stationary when she opened the door and that there was no warning from the guard. As once we accept that the train travelled considerably further than one would have expected, even on BRB's own case, it must follow that Mr Crookshank was being inattentive. If he was being inattentive, he could well have been inattentive in the crucial two second period before the train started moving. So what is the evidence? It is clear that the train can not have moved far, if at all, when she began to board....'

If at all? *If at all?*

CHAPTER THIRTY-SIX

Spinning The Wheel

Did I just hear my *own* QC say the train *may have moved*? I dug my nails hard into my thighs.

'...because Mr Crookshank said so in his interview and the train would soon have been moving too fast to have been boardable. Looking at the video it would have been moving too fast after four seconds hence the boarding point would be before the earliest point on BRB's braking tables. The fourth coach which she must have tried to board, would rapidly have been out of reach. So, if the train cannot have moved more than a few feet it is inexplicable why it should have taken so long to stop, again BRB's own braking tables and the evidence of Mr Hall illustrate this.

'So all the evidence points to the correctness of Miss Hill's version. That there was no contributory negligence. Even on Mr Crookshank's version, the inference is that he did not take action until too late – braking distances again and his statement to the police, show that he did not take action until Miss Hill had actually fallen. On balance of probabilities, earlier action would have prevented serious injuries. As these probably did not occur until she had been held by the platform and the running board for some time, it is likely she actually fell at the gap between the carriages. Either way, Miss Hill is the victim of serious breaches in safety rules and negligence through no fault of her own.'

So he got the guard to confess that his actions, or lack of them, allowed the accident to happen. But he dammed me in this final statement, suggesting that the train "may have moved". My own side suggesting that the train "may" have moved, was devastating. Surely this suggestion would lead the judge down the wrong path?

The High Court Judge put us out of our misery quickly.

'I consider that both the plaintiff and the guard were doing their honest best to present their versions of events in the best way they could. It is very difficult, as experience in these courts shows, for an honest witness to be an accurate one, especially when events move with very great speed and especially when those events are both to the injured party and to those involved in an accident, shocking and traumatic. It is, therefore, with no implication of moral blame or dishonesty, or anything of that sort, that I reach the conclusions that I do in this case. I do not, on the balance of probabilities, accept that the train was stationary when the plaintiff tried to board it.'

What?

'I am not satisfied that Mr Crookshank shouted a warning in time and I am not satisfied that if he did so the plaintiff heard it. I cannot on the other hand, like Mr Hall could not, conceive that Mr Crookshank delayed eight or nine seconds before taking emergency action in respect of the behaviour of a passenger, which I believe was taking place under his eyes, as he must have done had the plaintiff been trying to board a stationary train. That would be contrary to the training and instincts of a man whom I judge to be essentially a careful and conscientious man.'

What?

'What the plaintiff, as I judge it, was doing must happen time and time again on any busy suburban line, and I am not speaking now of people getting off while the train is still in motion, that happens more or less as a matter of course, I am speaking now of people trying to get on late when the train has begun to move. That being so, and indeed, Mr Crookshank acknowledged that it was so, the number of times that a train judders to a halt would be many if the emergency brake was applied every time. This no doubt explains, though it cannot in any sense excuse, in my judgment, what Mr Crookshank did, which was to wait and see, in his own words, "if the plaintiff made it". Accordingly there was a serious breach of the rules. A breach of a rule which was designed to protect passengers from potentially very serious danger. The delay in emergency braking amounted, not only to a breach, but also to negligence. On the other hand, the plaintiff put herself in a position of danger. She set the essential scene, she provided, to put it another way, the essential first ingredient without which her accident would not have happened.'

What?

'The delay in taking emergency action turned what probably would have been a relatively minor accident into the catastrophe that it was and it is thus that, weighing as best I can, the conduct of the parties concerned I reach the conclusion that the apportionment of liability in this case should be that I find 70% in favour of the plaintiff and I find that the defendants have proved 30% contributory negligence against the plaintiff. She will recover 70% of whatever her claim is. The amount of damages to which she will be entitled will be determined later.'

Though my first reaction was relief that we'd won, it was a strange kind of victory and it didn't take long for the anger to set in.

Outside the court I spotted my QC shaking hands with the opposition.

It's a game for them.

A game.

I was 30% responsible for boarding a moving train.

But the train had been still.

Stanley Hall, the railway expert, came to bid me an empathetic farewell. He said he thought that it had been a rough decision and this only compounded my anger.

The press were waiting at the High Court exit. Chasing us with cameras, insisting on a statement

Everyone was exhausted. The case has only lasted three days but all court cases are very emotionally draining. We celebrated – it was, in hindsight, an incredible victory – Diana vs the Goliath that was the all powerful British Rail, a young woman vs an enormous entity that was so well practised in legal matters.

The morning papers surmised that British Rail were mainly responsible because the guard hadn't applied the emergency brake, waiting to see if I "made it", and hadn't shouted a warning. But then, there it was again in black and white: I was "30% responsible for boarding a moving train".

My word against the guard, judged by one individual. I felt cheated. Why hadn't any details of the documents BR served, revealing the cover up and corporate bad behaviour ever come to light?

It all felt like part of a larger game – a governmental or even political game. Not to damn BR too greatly with privatization on the cards. To teach other commuters a lesson – not to rush for trains.

I hadn't been believed and it wasn't over by far. Next would come the actuary process and another court case. More pouring over events, repeat, repeat, repeat. Would I be able to I bear it?

If I'd known what was to follow, the answer to that question would certainly have been no.

The legal "game" was to continue for another four years. The ball was rarely in our court as British Rail set about raking over every single part of my career, my finances and my lifestyle past, present and future. Just how much was my life with legs worth?

Even though they were 70% liable, all sorts of tactics were employed, legal but inhumane to an extreme, to wear me down.

We'd won but I was the only one unable to walk. Away.

CHAPTER THIRTY-SEVEN

Vision Of Love

If I'd been in a full-time, salaried, job unable to work as I had before because of my injuries, they would have applied what's called an accelerator and a multiplier to extrapolate potential loss of earnings across my working years. I, however, was a self-employed woman, at the helm of a recently-formed company that was clearly going places.

The way the system works, it's necessary to extrapolate the likely needs of the future of a victim from the details of their past life and current situation: the difficulties they will have, the work opportunities, or lack of them, the need for extra care and equipment etc. right through to old age.

British Rail chose to go into every tiny detail of my life in minuscule argumentative detail. It was nothing short of horrific. An on-going onslaught of paperwork, interviews, claims, counter-claims, and endless stalling sprinkled with a nasty top layer of misogyny that stretched over the years into seeming infinity.

The legal system for compensation is designed to root out and destroy claims made by malingerers. When brutal damage has been done, and has, under the law, been proved to be done, the process of assault and battery some of the insurance companies are prepared to deliver leaves the injured feeling doubly injured and abused. Genuine claimants are pulverised by a minefield of experts, prodding for any loose cannons in a weakened psychological and physical state. It stinks. And has got even worse over the years as American-style ambulance chaser No Win No Fee lawyers fight each other in pursuit of the victims they can earn money from.

It felt like they were trying to get me to a place where I couldn't take it any more. Where I'd say OK that's enough, I give up. I reached that point on several occasions over those four years, but I was determined to never, ever give up. I just got more and more angry and determined that "justice" would win out. I'd lost that one in the courts already. My payment, whatever it turned out to be, would be reduced by 30% because the train *may* have been moving. Because I hadn't been believed. I hadn't lied. This deep, deep hurt continued to eat away at me throughout the process and remained for a long time.

The strain it put on my relationship with David was immense. But, before that came some respite. Immediately after the first trial and before it all began again, we took a special, restorative holiday in the Maldives. These were the days before artificial swim legs had been invented so David carried me, his "mermaid", to the beach every day to get into the sea. Our feelings and love for each other were further consolidated on that short break in paradise. We decided that he would move out of his fabulous flat in Cadogan Square and relocate to Tooting, next door to the knocking shop, until we could buy a house together.

Work was difficult. I couldn't even play at my full strength at straightforward business meetings. Most TV studios are simply warrens on different levels linked by high, rickety metal staircases. Whilst Soho, the traditional home for production company offices, is a jumble of tall, narrow buildings several stories high teeming with tiny corridors and no lifts.

However, we battled on and did our best to maintain the momentum. That autumn I went to France for MIPCOM. The narrow paths between the stands wouldn't take a wheelchair comfortably, and, despite the escalators, there was a lot of walking still to be done to reach people. I had been cast for three new pairs of limbs since the accident but none had proved suitable. I was still wearing the original pair of legs made for me 18 months earlier.

I would sit frustrated in a chair on the balcony outside the newsroom, directing Sarah with press releases and marketing ideas. When I did walk anywhere the pain and effort was apparent to all. Sarah did her best but she didn't have the same relationship with the clients, nor the same outgoing and inside knowledge that is so crucial to the public relations business.

On the eve of my birthday, David flew out to join me. We got up late the next day and went straight into a long boozy lunch. I brought up the subject of getting married. It felt natural and wholly right. I was so sad when he responded with an emphatic No that I sneaked off to the loo for a good cry.

As the day went on he seemed to get evermore cheerful as I became increasingly gloomy. Did I want to continue with someone like this?

That evening at our celebration dinner in the Hotel du Cap, David ordered asparagus and I ordered lobster. The waiter brought the raw asparagus to the table for David to approve, like it was a fish or a wine or something. He nodded at the plate. I thought that was a bit of an odd thing to do but didn't say anything. We were abroad. All sorts of minor rituals were done differently, especially in fancy French restaurants.

Then the waiter brought my plate and, with a flourish, opened the cloche lid to reveal a beautiful diamond ring resting on a white napkin.

David leant across the table. 'Diana, will you marry me?'

The tears arrived so full and furious I couldn't answer.

The maître d'hôtel appeared, 'What did she say?'

'She hasn't answered yet. Diana, will you marry me?'

'Yes!' I spluttered.

The asparagus had been a secret sign, a double-check that the ring should be presented.

Four months later we were holidaying on the Caribbean island of Grenada when I realised I was pregnant. We had gone out away from the hotel to a small fish restaurant for dinner. I love fish, but when the menu was handed to me, just reading about the different dishes made me want to gag. That's strange, I thought. Then I realised. I knew straight away what had happened. Fear of the future and how I would cope took hold. How would I walk when heavily pregnant? How could I walk?

The tremendous happiness and joy we shared that night and for the rest of our holiday soon overshadowed my worries and, for a short while, I let the practical challenges stay where they belonged, in the unknown future.

The hunt for a new home started in earnest.

The Occupational Therapist suggested Milton Keynes, a new town in the commuter belt, full of newly-built houses and manufactured open spaces.

'Lots of wheelchair-bound people are moving there,' she said helpfully. 'You'll feel right at home in no time!'

'Thanks.'

'You've got to think of the future, Diana. If you get anywhere with stairs, you will need a stairlift and believe you me, that', she pointed at my pregnant stomach, 'will be playing games with a stairlift.'

Spaciousness throughout for my wheels was a priority. We'd given up finding anywhere suitable in London and had extended our search to the pretty county of Hampshire. But then, on the day of my first scan, the day we both saw Lara for the first time, we viewed a beautiful riverside flat in

Barnes, South-West London. We couldn't believe how perfect it was, with parquet floors, broad corridors, massively wide doorways and direct access to a communal garden reaching down to the Thames. Finding that flat on that day, the day we had first seen our baby, was one of those wonderful, rare Meant to Be moments in life.

Maintaining an outward appearance of wholeness and completeness was of extreme importance to me but my energy to complete merely functional business tasks was draining away. Outwardly, by presenting a successful image, it was hard for people, even people close to me on a day-to-day basis like Sarah, to accept the reality of the excess energy expenditure in simply walking across a room, and the pain which accompanied it.

The clients' attitudes towards me had, at times, led to direct snubs so I'd been venturing out less and less. It felt like my role had been reduced to that of an office manager. Although Sarah had initially been very supporting of my position, tensions grew. People increasingly rang up to talk to Sarah – the now more visible side of the business.

Still, I battled on. What would I be without work? But then came the final straw.

I had arranged an intimate press event at The Dorchester, a hotel that catered admirably for my needs. I was "hand holding" at a press conference for a TV show starring Adam Faith and Zoe Wanamaker.

I'd pulled together some really good TV reviewers, previewers, feature writers and photographers. Knowing they weren't interested in Adam but wanted info on Zoe's life, I needed to address this imbalance. Zoe was in the bathroom of the hotel suite we'd hired for as a dressing room, getting made up. As I couldn't get inside the room to speak to her, I talked to her through the doorway.

'You might sense the journos asking a lot of questions to you,' I said. 'Could you defer whenever possible to Adam so that he doesn't feel too left out?'

Zoe readily agreed. As I'd forecast, every question at the conference was to Zoe. She deferred to Adam several times and everything went off smoothly. Absolute success. Or so I thought.

I returned to the now empty hotel suite to refresh myself and sort out my paperwork.

Adam, who'd previously made moves on me and been firmly rejected, stormed into the room with his flies undone.

'You fucking stupid bitch,' he snarled. 'I'll make sure you'll never work in this fucking industry again.' To my horror, he then positioned himself right over me with his crotch in my face and zipped his flies up. I couldn't defend myself. It was assault. Verbal rape. He ranted on, knowing full well I couldn't easily stand to defend myself.

Unbeknownst to me, Adam's chauffeur had been hovering in the hotel suite around the corner and had told him about my tip-off to Zoe. Select TV didn't stop working with us as it happened. But that was the nail in the press and PR coffin for me. If I'd been able-bodied it would never have happened. My normal instinct would have been to lean right into Zoe to whisper into her ear. Her make-up artist would never have said anything, discretion is a major part of their job description, every bit as important as being able to apply eyeliner in a straight line.

I decided to sell my half of the business to Sarah. With my pregnancy hormones coursing through my body, my energy was taxed to the limit simply getting there, parking the car and getting up to the office. Artificial limbs require frequent maintenance and adjustments, and ultimate replacement, on a semi-regular basis but even more so when you're pregnant. Roehampton Hospital was only open on weekday office hours. All my necessary appointments produced tensions between us which gradually worsened.

CHAPTER THIRTY-EIGHT

I Knew I Loved You

My dependency and need for help, from professionals as well as from David, friends and family naturally increased as the baby grew inside me. Because of the weight and balance problems, I had to go back to the wheelchair full time for the last few months of my term. At the same time David was having to adjust to severe difficulties at work where a 45% redundancy programme was doubling his workload. On top of which his American employers were completely certain he'd be retiring on my award amount! He kept trying to explain that unfortunately the UK damages system wasn't like America's, with its focus on punitive damages, but they wouldn't believe him. He was headhunted on a regular basis but didn't feel he could make the move with so much uncertainty in our lives.

To counterbalance these pressures he'd go off on regular skiing and fishing weekends. I knew he needed to keep sane and I encouraged him to go, but pregnancy hormones pack powerful emotional triggers and mine were all over the place. I felt abandoned every time.

Outwardly I carried on attempting to act the part others expected of me. The competent, together and powerful woman – mother hormones surging through my veins. A psychiatric report resulting from one of the several scrutinisations I had to undergo at British Rail's request, produced an interesting insight into this façade. Of how the façade can in itself lead to a lack of understanding by those around me of my actual needs. Thus reinforcing my vulnerability and isolation. Of how indeed some people actively resented my need for support.

I was highly sensitive to the way I was perceived by others and the difficulties they had coming to terms with my accident the first time they are told. I grew to expect the look of horror that comes across every single person's face. It's not quite the same but it's a bit like having to tell everybody new you meet that somebody's died over and over again. My way of helping them come to terms with my situation was to give an outward show of complete strength. Humour helped a lot, and still does, but you can't laugh 24 hours a day. Neither was I a depressed wreck 24 hours a day, not all the time, but the balance, the balance of normality was shot. Impending motherhood was a strong reminder that I would always be dependent on others – even if dependency is the skill of the prosthetists to fit the hardware systems that enabled me to walk.

I didn't stop working. I wrote features for MIP, MIPCOM & MIDEM publications with some success, doing profile pieces on industry executives living abroad. But it was only seasonal work, based around markets in Cannes. I applied to be a disabled model and for work on popular magazines like *Marie Claire* and *Eva*. Even with my good contacts the work was highly competitive and well-served by able bodied journalists.

I had to think carefully about the hospital. Which would be best equipped to deal with my special requirements for antenatal care, antenatal classes, parking, wheelchair access, equipment, delivery options and, top of the list, the understanding and attitude of the staff?

Towards the end of my pregnancy I was tired and almost constantly in pain. Activity in my uterus kicked off so much stump and phantom pain that the baby had to be induced. At first I was given the routine gas and air, but this was a calamity, zapping me, in a vivid flashback, directly to the day of the accident. When the midwife realised the screams had a top note of terror over the normal agonised cries of childbirth the mask was whipped from my face and an epidural speedily administered.

The unhappiest days of my life had been spent in hospital and now the happiest day of my life was also to be spent in hospital. I was choked with contentment that day. The moment I saw Lara, yowling and looking like the most exquisite skinned rabbit and put her into David's arms was, and will forever be, the best of my life. I thought I had experienced the very depths of love until I lay in that hospital bed with my baby by my side. I just stared at her in total wonder. Her beauty, and my sense of achievement at having produced such beauty, meant I was awake all night, such was the power of the good hormones coursing through my body.

A whole new set of practical problems opened up for me but for the most wonderful of reasons. Watching your child grow is one of the greatest wonders and privileges life can offer.

Her rapid development, the way she became increasingly active whilst I was so inactive, was a concern. Without work, my social circle gradually diminished. The friends I did see on a regular basis were my very close friends. Others had drifted away.

Balance is of great importance when wearing the false limbs. If I lose my total concentration for less than a second and a false foot hits a bump in the ground I will, without hesitation, fall over. The best way to imagine it is to be asked to walk on stilts that are going to crush your legs as you walk. For this reason, picking up Lara was dangerous and impossible. If I leant against a wall, and she held onto me without moving at all, it may have been conceivable. But she was an active child and as she squirmed all the time, this movement wasn't going to work. It was totally out of the question for me to ever attempt to walk with Lara in my arms. Except, thanks to technology, when swimming legs were invented and I could carry her in a swimming pool. Total bliss!

It was a constant hurt that some of the most natural, mothering gestures were denied to me – we had to have a nanny/housekeeper. Instead, I focused entirely on what I could do. Hugs, kisses, playing on the floor – and because it took me a while to get on the floor to play with Lara, her playtimes were frequently much longer perhaps than for an able-bodied person's baby.

David and Lara were my two spiritual legs – supporting me to the world. I had lost so much, but I really started to feel that I'd gained so much more. Perhaps I would have continued to feel like that if the great cloud of British Rail hadn't encroached on my life to such a massive degree, casting a dark shadow that can only be described as evil over those precious years of first motherhood. I was never, ever allowed to let some terrible memories fade as we set out to quantify and evaluate the worth of my life.

The first shock came in the shape of a supplementary psychiatric report by consultant psychiatrist, who we will call Mr Ragu.

As soon as Ragu was inside my flat he began to snoop around.

'Who is this lovely young woman?' he said, moving private papers on my bureau. A photo of me taken pre-accident was revealed.

'Me.'

'Oh.'

I later ripped to shreds every photograph of me with legs I could find.

His interview technique was appalling and, for a so-called psychiatrist, flimsy and insubstantial. He showed me very little respect through the course of the interview. His technique was punctured with sniggering (no doubt in an attempt to make me laugh) and insulting comments.

'Tell me about David. I suppose he is tall and very muscular.'

'Actually, he's the same height as me.'

'Same height as you BEFORE the accident you mean?'

Receiving a copy of that odious report was a tremendous blow: shoddy and shocking to the extreme. It contained inane, inaccurate remarks like "she was stressed by the loss of her leg". LEG! Singular!

It went on to say that, "perhaps for some time now, she has been trying to conceive. Perhaps since the autumn of 1991". Perhaps! A guess and a completely wrong one at that.

"Walks with the aid of one stick, some 18 months ago, about 100 yards.' Bad grammar and simply a lie. I haven't a clue where he got that information from. It was a total falsehood to imply that I could get around anywhere without the aid of 2 walking sticks, if not the wheelchair.

There was even a comparison to Douglas Bader. Bader was small, making it easier for him to wear false limbs. He was a man who had lost his legs in a war situation, making him a hero not a "trespasser" and he will have suffered none of society's sexual emphasis on "legs". He also had a very dutiful wife who looked after his special personal needs. Ragu's comparisons were fatuous and unacceptable.

The conclusion of the report was the biggest shock of all:

"The notes do suggest that she perhaps functions better than she admits during formal interviews and examinations".

So I was being knowingly deceptive now – ie lying. When all I wanted from the bottom of my heart was to be believed, that my life, who I was, what I had achieved to date, was worth something. If I hadn't been in such an overwhelming legal minefield at the time, a complaint to the official body of psychiatrists would have been wholly in order.

He couldn't have been more wrong. I was continually civil throughout those interviews and rarely broke down, which I was doing in "real" life all the time. None of the experts, hired by, and paid handsomely, by British Rail ever saw me in the depths of despair I had been in, and continued to endure as a direct result of the accident. In retrospect, if I'd been able to find any restorative humour beyond the anger I should have sent him a card from The One Legged Liar.

187

CHAPTER THIRTY-NINE

Part of Your World

Powerful memories of childhood would come flooding back at odd times. I identified strongly with Disney's *The Little Mermaid,* popular when Lara was small, longing for the "other world" but trapped in a body that wouldn't allow me access.

Wallace and Gromit in *The Wrong Trousers* was another film that Lara and I would watch together over and over again. Lara was Gromit, and I, when Wallace is forced to don his "wrong trousers", mechanical legs that took him where he didn't want to go, was Wallace.

I longed to be able to work effectively with people again. My career still meant everything to me, yet so many demands were coming in from British Rail I accepted that this next court battle, the amount of money I was "worth", was enough to be dealing with. I grew to dread the post and the ping of the fax machine. Beige envelopes from Cooper's would appear regularly with more news, mostly bad. Dealing with it all had become, once more, a full-time job.

I had to write a full statement, an account of my life, my needs, past and future, which in the end came to nearly 20,000 words. Without knowing it I was gradually becoming a writer, as well as a journalist. Ironically what I'd always wanted to be.

One of the biggest challenges was gathering in comprehensive witness statements to show how MediaVision had been affected by my accident. The company had struggled on after I left, but the clients dwindled away and Sarah eventually called it a day. Before my accident, MediaVision had been growing fast and would have been a force to reckon with in the industry, but they weren't going to take my word for it. I had the embarrassing job of seeking out working character references from everybody I could think of who we'd had close dealings with.

188

The awful shame of having to go, cap in hand, for references from major players in the TV industry, some of them very close friends, who barely had time to think or drink a cup of coffee let alone sit down and write about me, was counterbalanced by the ringing endorsements which came through as to my professional abilities and strength of character. It was bittersweet. What might have been.

All of this was getting me more and more down. When David's work schedule finally became less frantic, we decided the time was right to get married.

We settled on our favourite place, the South of France. David had been married, briefly, before so we had a register office wedding on David's birthday, and then, a month later, a big blessing at the 14th Century seafront Château de la Napoule.

Our local vicar liaised with an English vicar living in Cannes so the blessing was like a full English church ceremony. Over 80 family and friends came out, we arranged accommodation for them and I got a special deal with the airline. Ten-month-old Lara was our bridesmaid.

It's funny to look back on it now, but it was quite a business to arrange all the details of the wedding, catering etc by phone and fax. In French as well of course, so it all felt extremely risky. On top of which, we decided we'd have a grand fancy dress ball on the eve of the wedding as well.

The logistics of organising it all were off the scale. Having organised a weekend of flights, accommodation, all meals and entertainment for over 85 people, there were bound to be a few hitches. But the only problem emerged on our way to Heathrow airport in the taxi.

'I am a list fanatic as you now know David, but I have forgotten something. Something important..'

'Stop fretting, Di, you've done a wonderful job, it's all sorted.' He patted my hand, and lovingly touched my engagement ring.

'Stop! Driver, turn round.' I suddenly squealed. 'We have to go back.'

'We can't,' David protested. 'We'll miss our plane!'

'I've forgotten my wedding dress!'

We still made the flight, despite the detour.

All the work involved for our wedding however, was in glorious contrast to the other kind of stress and worry. Instead of analysing how much I was worth as a human, I revelled in arranging one of the most wonderful events us humans can enjoy.

The fancy dress theme for the big pre-wedding eve bash was Great Lovers of the World. Everyone pulled out all the stops for this. We had a fantastic mixture of characters from Antony & Cleopatra to Lois Lane & Superman. David and I were *The Addams Family* characters Gomez & Morticia with Lara as Pubert. It was a wonderful night of happiness and laughter, so much laughter. I got to bed at 4.30am only to be woken by the baby at 6.30. All eighty of us took our hangovers to a wedding breakfast, stylishly presented as only the French can. Thankfully I'd cleverly arranged the wedding to be at 6pm so there was time for recovery before the next round of celebrations.

The ceremony was topped and tailed with fireworks and Wagner's *Ride of the Valkyries* which caused such a stir locally they all thought, along with red carpets laid out in the grounds of the castle, that a royal wedding was taking place.

The blessing was so special, in the sunshine, surrounded by flowers with the chateau as a backdrop on one side and far-reaching views down over the glittering sea on the other. It felt like a fantasy, surpassing by far those drug-fuelled waking dreams I'd had in my hospital bed. I'd dreamed of a fairytale wedding and it's exactly what happened.

Dreams sometimes do come true. David's speech, delivered under those glorious plane trees at the five course French banquet, was incredible, producing tears of laughter as he regaled funny stories from my childhood, to tears of emotion as he raised a toast, to me, 'Our best friend, my beautiful wife.' For a whole day afterwards I couldn't stop crying. From happiness.

After the fairytale wedding we lived happily ever after. Well, no. As in all fairy tales....

CHAPTER FORTY

Back to Life

There followed a time of brinkmanship, high emotion, inappropriate games, depression, frustration and incredible anger as both my past and my future were put under the closest scrutiny.

Life became frozen. Everything had to be measured against the future, unknown, date of the hearing.

There were periods of lull, periods of intense activity, small interventions, major interventions, complete insults, avoidance tactics, shock letters arriving in the post and shock phone calls out of the blue sprinkled with visits from lawyers, doctors and psychiatrists. This drip drip effect went on for three years before reaching an intensity for the final eight months.

I had to rely on my legal team to clarify the information and explain the legal dance they were going through. A lot of it didn't make any sense at all. The cruelty and unfairness of the system, the sheer lack of basic humanity in the behaviour of some of the people involved would have been intriguing if it hadn't been so tragic.

The maximum claim for amputation at that time was £20,000 (around $29,700). This harked back to the early 19th century. The laws have been changed now but at the time we had no choice but to adhere to those figures. To get me a decent settlement we had to concentrate on "future loss of earnings" and "pain and suffering". Pain and suffering amounts can be massive but in order to prove them I had to relive them.

The first big task was my Schedule of Loss. I was asked to provide details documenting the cost of, big breath: motoring expenses, wheelchair expenses, clothing receipts, oil/skincare preparations, prescriptions, dry cleaning and laundry, holiday costs, counselling, physiotherapy, personal trainer, nanny service, housing costs, carpet care, locksmith, tax returns, invoices, sale of shares to Sarah, future loss of earnings, future loss of benefits in kind, a breakdown of my care report, future care childcare, future possible child, cost of employing mother's help when children aged between 5-10; future cost of domestic help with heavier tasks, domestic help when children 10-15, later years care as physical abilities deteriorate, additional cost of transport, adaptation of vehicle, additional mileage directly due to disability, additional car insurance, fitting hand controls to new cars every 3 years, walking sticks, quickie wheelchair, powered outdoor wheelchair, all-terrain vehicle, wheelchair ramp, bath, supportive chair, minor gadgets – cooking baskets, raised laundry storage basket, lightweight table trolley, cost of installing additional static telephone lines, cordless phone, additional cost of childcare equipment, cost of long handled gardening tools, later in life assistance with lifting, shower chair with amputee axle plate, replacing redundant wardrobe, additional cost of clothing, excessive wear and tear, replacement of redundant footwear, essential oils, prescriptions vitamin supplements, towels, heating, modifying flat, modifying future family home. Oh and with receipts please, or proof of estimate.

When that was done it was on to full MediaVision business accounts for the past three years.

Then another letter came requesting more detail regarding the difficulties that we both experienced when taking holidays.

Then I had to get statements from all of MediaVision's clients.

Then the come-backs on my Loss of Earnings statement started to arrive.

They didn't accept that additional staff were required or that it was necessary for David to accompany me on trips.

They suggested that I could quite possibly still work in the TV industry, what with all my contacts there. Or I could become a fundraiser, a market researcher, or do "trades exhibition work" whatever that meant. Demonstrating wheelchairs at medical trade fairs I suppose.

In the summer of 1995 we finally limped forwards towards a settlement in a one step forward, three steps backwards kind of way. There was so much to do, so much to prepare that my whole life became my fight.

I kept a diary during the build-up, recording the frustrations and agonies of it all.

BR's first counterclaim was that I'd need an electric chair and a couple of sticks and, for my loss of earnings, £11,000, (around $16,300), should do me nicely. This all smacked of the opening bid in a Turkish bazaar for a moth-eaten old carpet and was easy to laugh at.

Most dealings with the legal system are, at the best of times, fraught with pressures and tension. The process of buying a house, even when the sale is smooth, is, you'll know if you've ever done it, full of tension. Here the stakes were so much higher. I found myself fighting people who were actively in the business of not wanting me to have a future and who didn't care how long it took or how much it cost to defeat me. The frustrations came at me from both ends, from BR but also from my own side.

In early June I was in the house on my own again, feeling isolated and very fed up because my solicitor Steve had gone off on his holidays without telling me.

There must be something in law school about this – don't tell your clients you're going away or they'll all pounce on you at once. I knew I wasn't his only client but I felt totally impotent.

He finally phoned at 6pm on the day of his return, by which time I was feeling like a complete afterthought. 'We've got them on the run, Di,' were his words. My doom turned to elation, but only briefly because I knew there'd be a come-down to follow, if not that day then the next, if not the next then the following day.

David and I were thinking of making a complete change when it was all finally over, and started house hunting outside London. I remember especially a house in Andover. It was totally unsuitable because I couldn't face the stairs. I felt such a bloody cripple and I envied the owner. She had four children and a career from home. I found myself wondering for a moment if perhaps I could have another baby.

It didn't last long for I'd lost my ability to look forward to the future. I had finally relented to my poor brain's chemistry and had succumbed to my GP's advice – a mild antidepressant. It helped to calm and conceal, to cement the tears that threatened to erupt at any time. I had to be strong, for Lara most of all, for David, my family, for me. I longed to feel healthy again but lost the will to hope that I ever would.

CHAPTER FORTY-ONE

This Wheel's On Fire

Every day from April up until the final court case in July there seemed to be a further development that had to be acted upon. There was some good news on the compensation side – all multipliers were raised. This was due to a change in the law. The legal system had finally admitted that personal injury claims have been far too small and plaintiffs had been running out of money too quickly. It wouldn't have happened had the case been settled earlier.

Then the You Should letter arrived. A long, frightening missive from our own solicitors, pages and pages of it, telling us what we had to do, each paragraph starting "you should..." which made us feel weak and exhausted just reading it.

They wanted a comprehensive statement outlining the effects of the accident on my personal and professional life, both before and after I lost my legs. They wanted details of the pain, discomfort and inconvenience.

They wanted an in-depth history of MediaVision. How, why and when I set the company up, what clients I had at the time of the accident and where I felt the business was going. I had to outline the effect on the business that the accident had had, where the company was going in the future and where I saw it going with Sarah running the business on her own. What were the differences between the company's profile now and the company's profile before the accident?

They wanted a comparison of my role in the company to Sarah's before the accident.

They wanted details of the clients that made up the business at the time of the accident and the prospects with each client for the future. Which clients were mine and which Sarah's? How did I feel each client would have contributed to the growth of MediaVision if the accident hadn't happened?

They wanted a detailed account of my accommodation history from a year before the accident to the present date and future views about accommodation, outlining any particular needs and requirements. I had to describe what help about the house I needed now and would need in the future, highlighting particularly difficult tasks.

They wanted details of the problems I'd had during pregnancy/birth and generally on a day to day basis in bringing up Lara.

They wanted details of my lovers. I had to mention my relationship with Andrew and how it was before and after the accident. How I met David and the relationship that I'd built with him. They even wanted to know about our rows! Termed as "highlighting any difficulties there have been between us brought about as a result of the accident". Counselling, antidepressants, and the effects of all had to be mentioned.

I had to explain travelling problems, car insurance, parking, the hiring of two taxis for mine and Lara's gear every time we went away. How I coped with gardening, decorating, the ongoing treatment at Roehampton for the rest of my life and what treatment I'd had since the accident. I had to devote a section to my leisure needs like Quad Biking and swimming legs etc.

David also had to prepare an extensive statement dealing with both his work and private life. All this was intrusive to a paranoia-inducing level. Each time I left the flat I looked up and down the road, imagining I would catch the legal defence video camera "spies" in action. Were they recording how far I could walk, did I really need the nanny, carrying my precious baby? Just how much shopping can one woman do? The British Rail quantum defence team were dogged. They were, ironically, trespassing deep into my life. Perhaps I would counter sue them for trespass.

We had to prepare a video film showing "a day in the life of Diana Morgan" showing all the difficulties I had. If we found this too difficult to manage we should instruct a professional videographer. Ideally the video should highlight some of the more difficult tasks I encountered on a day to day basis, like getting on the floor to play with Lara, getting up in the middle of the night to go to the toilet or to look after Lara and putting my legs on in the morning. Diana, the movie. Bring it on!

They wanted yet more details of loss beyond the Schedule of Loss I'd already gone through, with, yet more, receipts. This part was really urgent.

In the same letter I was told they were getting a report from my GP but wanted me to be seen again by the psychiatrists and that they would be contacting Andrew and Sarah. Signing off they asked if I could "attend to those various matters as quickly as possible".

And that was from my own side.

I set about phoning up past contacts and clients of MediaVision to ask them to write personal statements or be interviewed. All agreed but it was highly embarrassing. Contributors included TV and film people Colin McKeown, Michael Winner, Richard Leworthy, Julian Newby, and my colleagues Barbie Holloway, Christine Aziz, Chris Mould, Maria Morgan, Jane Harbord, Tony Barrow and, of course, Sarah.

Some of the statements, professional, domestic and medical were disputed, though, and more detail called for. Ridiculous detail at times.

The arrival of their counter-schedule, the response to our claim, with yet another long list of requirements, was one of the worst shocks of the process. It showed what we were dealing with: a real, full-on, bloody fight to the death. Our claim had been reduced by 7/8ths. That was the gap we were dealing with. I gave Steve merry hell and wanted to threaten the press but Steve pleaded with me not to, going off on one of his straighter "game" analogies.

'It's a game, Di. Please play it.'

'It's not a level playing field, Steve. I've been crippled for life.' I shouted, slamming the phone down. When I finally calmed down I set to writing my reply. All 10 pages of it.

They'd left it until the very last minute – "close to the legal bone" as Steve put it. Off on his game terminology again. He really did sound pleased with the way things were going at that point and it rubbed off on me. I didn't care if it wasn't settled and we went to court. I was angry. Angry enough to take it into court and Steve didn't disagree. But he wanted to wait to see what they would come up with. He reckoned they were running around like headless chickens.

Every little dance the lawyers played together, at my expense, shredded my nerves a little more. At one point they wanted me to bring into court all the clothing receipts for extra clothing I needed because the metal legs rubbing against the wheelchair made holes in my trousers and skirts.

I'd get sudden fits of anger and would erupt into the most colourful stream of swearwords I could come up with – the kind that used to trot out of my mouth back in my post-accident Brett times.

196

To cheer myself up one day, I re-read everybody's statements. Michael Winner's was over the top – "Previous to this vile accident, this incredible woman would have been paid £100,000 (around $148,300) a year by working with me on my films." He was so looking forward to his day in court, bless him.

Julian Newby: "The PR industry in the media certainly is a growing one and MediaVision would have had more than its share of that growth if Diana had been able to keep going. I have sadly observed MediaVision's slow decline since Diana left. I still have contact with it, it issues the odd press release, but it is no longer a PR company which springs instantly to mind when I require certain help, expertise or advice."

Tony Barrow (PR for The Beatles and Cilla Black, Editor in Chief for all the MIDEM magazines covering some 8 markets over in Cannes): "It would be impossible for Diana to keep up with her clients on location in the wake of her accident. With the best will in the world she would find the physical demands of the work overwhelming and these are not functions which a principal can delegate."

Colin McKeown: "Diana was a major star in her chosen field of PR, certainly within the top ten percent but the industry will never be an even playing field. It's an industry that serves the false god of "image", and given Diana's horrendous injury, a door has very unfortunately closed on that part of her career."

Richard Leworthy, Director Primetime Television, our biggest client: "Sarah will no longer manage our account from May as we are moving to another PR firm who will be paid three times as much. This would not have been the case had Diana not had the accident. I believe MediaVision would have gone to be even more successful. Together as a team Diana and Sarah were effective, but Diana was the dynamic force."

I'd proved my will and determination from my previous life, but then I began to wonder if that might not go against me. What if I were penalised for it? Were they watching me? I truly started to think that every closed-in van that parked in the road contained a BR surveillance team! I started to give running commentaries to myself on myself like, "returned from car after being absent from home all day. Didn't take wheelchair with her".

It was all about money of course. The irony was I'd never been a money-oriented person. How I longed to return to more important concerns. But I couldn't. Then I thought about the possible publicity. Could I bear it? Or what if there wasn't any? Could I bear that?

Steve insisted I got Andrew as a witness. I didn't want to and explained, as best as I could, to a man, why. Steve's take was that Andrew would feel OK about giving a statement in order to redeem himself. I didn't think so somehow.

The pace heated up. We had a QC on board, a small, stocky and direct chap. I was impressed. At the same time British Rail moved their legal and insurance dept over to one of the biggest defence firms in the country. They were known for their unpleasant attitudes and cruel manner, citing Steve to explain them as "lower than a snake's hip" on more than one occasion. For example, their way of asking Sarah to reveal all documents to do with MediaVision was to inform her that she would go to prison if she didn't do so.

There was a flurry of intense activity before the final schedule of losses was sent to British Rail's lawyers. Steve kept phoning me for vital pieces of information to fill in the gaps. Bits and pieces on lifts, clothes, holidays etc. The total amount in the schedule came to nearly £1.7 million (around $2.5 million). I was heartened by the amount but wary of getting too enthused.

Then the defence started stalling. This, I was told, was standard practice for a defence firm. Under the boundaries of the law they were allowed to do this.

It all turned into a waiting game. Steve said that if he was a betting man, he would estimate that BR would come in at half the 70% loss ie £1.1 million halved is £600,000 which would be negotiated upwards to about £750,000 (around $1,100,000). That's what he would take his bet on, if British Rail got all their tackle together which of course they would.

Whilst we were still waiting for payment into court – which would reveal the extent of their bluff, or not – the footballer Graham Souness was awarded £750,000 damages for being called a dirty rat! This was later reduced on appeal but the timing couldn't have been worse for my state of anxiety.

The only distraction was my darling Lara. Just loving her, laughing with her, holding her as much as I could when I wasn't upset. It wasn't much more than a distraction because we couldn't make any kind of decision until it was all over. The call finally came from Steve. They'd sent the counter schedule. His voice sounded flat and my stomach dropped. They hadn't put any payment into court which surprised him. Their counter claim amounted to some walking sticks and an electric wheelchair.

After yet more legal stalling, they eventually came up with a far more detailed counter claim. Michael Winner phoned, putting the wind up me even more but making me laugh as usual. 'My darling, it's becoming a gambling game. My mother would have loved it.'

Another process was the subpoena, where witnesses are called into court. Michael was to be one of my powerful character witnesses who'd agreed to be cross-examined. Another friend, Richard, phoned me to say he couldn't make it because he'd be on holiday. Steve went berserk.

'He has to Di! He's been subpoenaed!'

'In that case,' I told him. 'We'll have to fly him back.'

Unreality was starting to settle in beside disbelief.

We were finally told the sum into court would be £631,708.55 (around $934,000).

The day this "offer" came in, I had phoned David to let him know. He returned from another hard day at the office, looking pale and distracted.

Eventually, he spoke.

'I have just had to agree to a bonus to a young buck, a talented trader, but he's an idiot. A 27 year old. He will fritter the money.'

'How much,' I asked, feeling nauseous.

'£650,000'.

I didn't like it being referred to as compensation. What was I being compensated for? I called it blood money. Replace my energy? My mobility? My naturally buoyant, positive way of thinking? They couldn't.

If the High Court deemed BR correct in assessment, if the judge came in at one penny below the offer from British Rail, then I would have to pay all court costs which would be £15,000/day (around $22,000) for the barristers alone. I was endlessly reminded that depending on the "type" of judge we got, most of the male judges would deem me in a very comfortable position, financially, married to someone that worked in the banking industry. I failed to ask the question, "but what if we get divorced?". I didn't think it was a possibility.

Steve went into overdrive with his analogies, taking it "to the wire" with "brinkmanship". They briefly took over from his football jargon, at least. I'd long since turned all the gaming terminology into a joke. I looked up brinkmanship in the dictionary: "the art or policy of pursuing a dangerous course to the brink of CATASTROPHE before desisting".

I was told it wouldn't be a court case of 3 days but more like 10 days, and those costs would be in the region of £100,000 (around $148,000) and that was what I stood to lose. My instinct was f**k'em. What's £100K when I had to live with my gross losses?

Then I was told that court cases adjourn at the end of July so we'd all have to return in October!

This was the final straw for David and he gave up the fight.

I didn't. It was me against all of them.

They wanted to question me again. They arrived at 11am and stayed until 5.

We'd prepared a video of my daily life as requested. It was graphic and visually close to the edge on the difficulties I had to endure day in day out every day. Helen's boyfriend Jonny had done a good job. I'd written the script and done the voice-over. It all looked very professional. "You should see videos of babies with brain damage" was one of the comments from my legal team. Followed by comments comparing my career to Edina's in *Absolutely Fabulous*. Followed by how lucky I was to have such a good earner for a husband.

I hated all of them at that moment. Steve for not telling me some crucial points, the other two for being so legal and defensive. I felt like I'd lost my team.

CHAPTER FORTY-TWO

You Can't Always Get What You Want

Looking back, as I was continually being asked to, only clarified the fact that my whole life had been filled with work. Now I was in the unsatisfying position of being given a bit of money to compensate for what was lost when the losses were so little to do with money. For me it was all about my loss of mobility, a freedom of movement that had translated to an energy for life, and the termination of my career. I'd worked so hard to get into the position I was in. I'd thrived on knowing large numbers of people and getting people together. The spread of my contacts had diminished enormously. People who had once meant a great deal to me had dwindled away in my life, although not in my mind. I started to feel isolated and cut off from life and turned more and more to reading.

The suitability of my own witnesses were questioned by my own team.

Could calling Michael Winner go against us?

Sarah was actually approached by British Rail to stand for them!

My own side started picking away at our statement and subtracting figures, piece by piece. Subtracting things I'd obviously need in the future. I slowly started to sink into a state of shock. I began attacking them in a subtle way. I remained calm and reasonably friendly but I could have quite willingly strangled them at times. When their figures then matched the oppositions to within a £1,000 (around $1,500) I could have died from shock. It looked to me like they weren't prepared to fight. They didn't think my claim was worth all the work we'd put in.

I had to have another going over by a psychiatrist. By the time David and I got there through London traffic I was feeling very sick in the head. That point is probably the closest I've ever come to a nervous breakdown. The psychiatrist was utterly hopeless. He took the unforgivable "does she take sugar" route, ignoring my eye contact and asking David questions like 'Well, how has she been?' It was unbelievable.

When the psychiatrist left the room to get me an ashtray, David turned to me and whispered 'it's Mr Bean!' Tears turned to giggles. We were only there for about 15 minutes and left, disgusted with him. All he did was advise me on some different types of antidepressants to the Prozac I was already on. His charge was probably something like £1,000 (around $1,500) or even more for writing his crappy report. I started having visions of hidden cameras to expose these people.

Steve called to say they'd had the "How Far Apart Are We?" call.

The depths of my crisis reached, I became inured to it all, because I had to be. When you hit the bottom and the next bit of bad news comes in it starts to wash over you. It's like your emotions go on strike and you start observing your life almost as if it's a movie. Automatic pilot took over some roles as my natural strength rallied for the final punch of the fight.

I was subpoenaed and would have to appear in court to testify the strength of my business and abilities previous to the accident. Steve was, at least, back to calling the lawyer on the other side a vicious bastard, which made me feel I was on the same side as Steve again. Good news! That's how it got.

'You shouldn't have to suffer all this, Di, not twice,' he said.

'Just tell me, is it going to turn out OK in the end?'

Their counter offer was about £600,000 (around $888,000). If I were to live for another 50 years, that would be £14,000 (around $20,700) a year. Hardly living comfortably. Especially not as my brain was forever calculating just how much my disability was costing me... Did we fight them? Why did I have to keep fighting them? Why when I was the victim? I was tired of fighting. How many lies had they told? How much had they spent fighting me? How much on litigation and legal fees instead of just compensating me for their... their incompetence? Why couldn't they just say sorry and get on with it? I wanted the full amount, I wanted them to pay for what they did to me.

But that's not how it worked. If I didn't accept their offer and left it to the judge to decide the compensation there was a big a risk. If I was awarded a single penny **less** than BR had offered then I would be liable to pay the legal fees and costs. As effectively they would have compensated me for more than the award was worth. I'd lose everything.

David and I went out to the pub and I started, unconsciously, to work on him. Explaining how our side were trying to close the deal without a last fight. It felt to me like it was all boys together. Having been told earlier that the opposing QC was an absolute vicious bastard, they now described him as "polite but thorough".

There was a sexist element in all of it too. "She's married to a banker, what does she need with more money?" The worst sexism came from a woman, in the defence legal team, who claimed that there was no way I would be "having a baby and gallivanting around Cannes as she used to". She had tried to say that Sarah worked part time. Steve got very cross with her. All I could remember was Sarah, glowing, with her neat pregnancy bump at 6 months, skipping off to the market in Cannes, while I lay, couch prone, aching all over, patting my pregnant stomach in a desperate attempt to calm myself at our differing situations.

David said the sensible thing was to take the money, put it behind us and forget about it sooner rather than later.

But I couldn't do that. I was livid. After a fitful night, I phoned Michael Winner and burst into tears. In total contrast to his public persona, his tone was kindly.

'I can't give you advice on such an important decision. I'll have to get hold of my lawyer.'

Michael tracked down his QC and got straight back to me. He said it sounded like a reasonable offer, carefully worked out to appeal to a "tight-arsed" judge but that we should definitely have one last go at them. This gave me the strength to write a stinking letter to Steve saying I wasn't going to accept it and that they should revise their offer or I would go to court. I faxed it and didn't phone him.

They were all waiting for me to take the payment and I wasn't going to. I took Michael Winner's lawyer's advice and dug my heels in. Steve came into his own then. He got his boxing gloves out and prepared to take it to the wire. If I wanted to give up at any time, he said, if I wasn't sleeping and couldn't bear the strain then just one phone call would settle it. He was a gambling man, clearly. He liked the video, called me a real TV star. Sarky, but truthful. He moved on from sporting analogies to card games.

'We are not bluffing – but will they hold?'

The game. The tactics. The gambling. From my strength at the bottom of my wits' end, I couldn't help but admire it. It was incredible.

The deadline came and went and my nerves were back up to full edge tension. The game had become underhand. The bastards were playing dirty tricks. They offered a couple of extra grand for a gagging order – restraining me from ever talking about the case. Steve even agreed with my publicity threats. 'I hope you get them splashed all over the papers now, Di. They deserve to be slapped around the face.' He sounded so defeated that I started telling him jokes to cheer him up.

The wire we'd taken it to was fraying. We discovered their QC, whilst acknowledging that the case would run for more than 5 days, had booked himself a holiday.

It looked like they never intended to go to court. If it *did* run on it would either be adjourned or I'd get a Top Silk judge instead of a High Court judge. This wasn't so good. QCs are more likely to be cautious because they're not as experienced.

The edgy, underhand games continued.

They wanted to know who filmed our video, on what dates, and who produced it. They wanted all clothing receipts (the delightful lady). One of their side actually turned up at Coopers to look at motoring receipts.

Steve sounded so low when he phoned me with all of this news that I arranged for an Interflora bunch of flowers to be sent to him with the message,

"They think it's all over. It is now! England in Germany, World Cup 1966."

He responded with the message, "There's still some players on the pitch, Di."

In other words the QCs were still battling it out.

The delaying tactics continued and my nerves escalated to breaking point.

We took it all the way to the day before we were due in court. That's when we'd find out, mid-afternoon, who the judge was going to be.

One judge.

That's what it all boiled down to. Who would it be? The man who was to deem what my life was worth after all my hard work. What kind of a character was he? What mood would he be in that day? How had his bacon and eggs been that morning? Any burnt toast?

We found out, mid-afternoon, that we had a "good guy". Our QC said I'd make a good impression in front of him.

Steve phoned to say he believed them when they said there'd be no additional money full stop. David broke off from work, came home, got down on his knees in front of me and begged me to accept the money.

In my heart I absolutely wanted to put it before the judge. I desperately wanted to tell British Rail that no, that is not enough for the damage they had done to me. My spirit was willing but I had to accept that I was worn out.

We all were.

I accepted the money. On the virtual steps of the court – via a phone call to Steve, in tears, but again, relieved beyond measure.

I had been advised not to specify exact amount I received at the time. The ridiculous legal discrepancies between amounts awarded to those that have been libelled and those who have lost limbs, with figures having to comply with archaic laws, was uppermost in my mind. That, at around this time my husband David was OKing £650,000 bonuses to 25 year old bankers only compounded my disbelief. My comment to the huddle of press waiting outside the courtroom was:

'I received more than Jason Donovan was awarded for being called "a queer" and considerably less than Graeme Souness was awarded for being called "a dirty rat".'

What I wanted to say to the press that day from the bottom of my heart was that what I'd just been put through should never have been allowed to happen to anybody. Ever.

The Press reported the next day:

A young mother's courage and determination as she learnt to walk again were praised by a High Court judge yesterday. Diana Hill had both legs amputated, one below the knee and one above, after a guard delayed applying the emergency brake because he 'waited to see if she made it' resulting in her falling down to the tracks beneath the train. Mr Justice Wright praised the way she had dealt with her "most appalling injuries" and awarded her substantial damages. Soon after the accident Ms Hill read in a newspaper that she could be facing prosecution by Transport Police who were considering taking the action under an 1898 bylaw, under which she could have been fined £50. British Rail have not issued an apology, either publicly or personally to Ms Hill.

It was later revealed that BR had spent over a million pounds (appx $1,500,000) on legal fees.

EPILOGUE

What You Do With What You've Got

You may have found parts of *Love & Justice* harrowing to read. I have certainly had great difficulty at times in the writing of it. It has come to me in batches – the first third written on the upsurge of energy following the end of the court case. A literary agent was secured, but my words came to a grinding halt when my dear dad died. The second third followed a couple of years later, buoyed up as I was by the most wonderful of weeks on an Arvon Foundation course at Totleigh Barton. One of the tutors, Livi Michael said at the time: 'You may find you take a very long time to write the whole of this book. The themes are very big.' And how right she was. The final, and for me, most difficult third of the book, was only recently completed.

I don't regret this protraction however, for my true justice in the face of such devastation has been to live a full, and at times, rather wonderful life.

Some may have dwelt on the "What if's". I did not have that luxury. I had to face up to the new me, the resurrected Diana and get on with it. And, gradually the what if's became and have become, "I never would have done's"…including, two years as CEO for the Limbless Association, where I set up the ALI fund to help secure the future for Ali Abbas, who lost his entire family and both his arms, along with his friend, Ahmed Hamza, who lost a leg and arm, at the start of the Iraq war in 2003. I have counselled many amputees over the years, including Martine Wright and Gill Hicks, whose own lives and bodies were ripped apart by the terrorist London underground tube bombings of 2005. I hope I have helped all these people as much as I was helped by my closest friends who made me laugh all those years ago. And hope this book will perhaps help others to see that, whilst it may feel like it at the time, their lives are indeed not over when sudden trauma and tragedy hits.

Previous to the accident, I had been fit, but not sporty. Eight years after I had Lara, persuaded by a Wheelchair Tennis friend, I turned to the sport, and within a year of solid training, was playing at international tournament level. This activity, in turn, helped me to get to the finals of *Dancing On Wheels*, a BBC programme in the *Strictly Come Dancing* vein, where us wheelie dancers were paired with previous celebs from SCD. Such fun, and culminating in my tango-ing with Boris Johnson in front of County Hall, and dancing in the Paralympics Opening Ceremony.

There have been many more highlights over the years, circumstance and events I could never in my wildest dreams as a very young girl, have ever begun to imagine. What I did want then, from about the age of seven onwards was to be a writer. And to live by the sea.

Well, hello....?

PHOTOGRAPHS

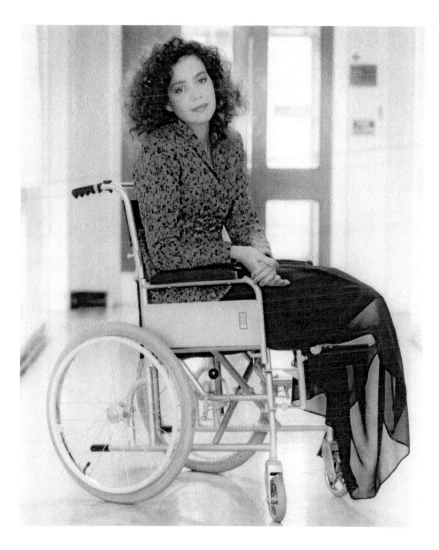

Very 1980s model

Seeking fame and fortune: singing with local group

Young Love: with Duncan on Hampstead Heath

With Paddy and Duncan, Cornwall

Horse riding with Andrew in the Cotswolds

First day out of hospital with Andrew

With David

After the High Court case, with David in the Maldives

Married at The Château de la Napoule, South of France

Lara and her mummy

PICTURE CREDITS

ACKNOWLEDGEMENTS

Deep gratitude and respect to all those who saved my life at St George's Hospital, Tooting, London and to all the surgeons, doctors, and especially the nurses and rehabilitation staff at Queen Mary's Hospital, Roehampton, London.

Love and thanks to my 'readers/encouragers': Ian Comerford, Viv 'Vivalatta' Greenwell, Jane Harbord, Rosie Jones, Dinah May, Neil Thomas, and my darling Mum, Agnes Veen Hill. (A prolific reader until the last few months of her life, this book, in pre-edit form, was the last book she read. Although some of the content was very distressing for her, she loved it and declared, with such pride: 'My goodness, you really can write.' She passed away April 2014).

Thank you to the authors Susie Kelly and Diane Chandler, for both the sterling work they have done on the beta-reading of this book, and for their amazing feedback.

So much love and thanks go to my sister, Helen, brother David, and brother in law, Jonny Clothier, for being there, throughout.

And to Stephanie Zia, publisher at Blackbird Digital Books. Thank you so much for your patience, for keeping the faith in my story, and for delivering it, as promised...

Keep up to date with all Diana Morgan-Hill news and new titles, join the Diana Morgan-Hill Mailing List:
http://eepurl.com/bip13v

(All email details securely managed at Mailchimp.com and never shared with third parties.)

AUTHOR PROFILE

Writing has been at the heart of Diana's working life. She was a press and publicity manager for *Brookside*, Channel 4's soap opera, and ITN and then became a journalist and editor for a number of TV business publications. After freelancing for the MIDEM organisation, she set up MediaVision, a press, public relations and strategy consultancy to cater for the booming markets in international television. Suffering from catastrophic injuries following a train accident, she then had to refocus and has subsequently worked as a TV presenter, as a chief executive, was MD of a small publishing company, and an assistant producer in TV. Her voluntary work has included trustee and committee positions for the National Wheelchair Tennis Foundation, The Limbless Association and the British Red Cross. She now supports the Arvon Foundation, a charity that provides writing weeks for potential authors, and she continues to counsel others suffering from limb loss. Diana lives in Dorset, by the sea. She is a motivational speaker and is presently writing her first novel, a psychological thriller.

If you have enjoyed this book please would you consider leaving a short review at Amazon.com; Amazon.co.uk; Waterstones.com (UK) or www.barnesandnoble.com (US)? Online reviews really do make all the difference to the life of a new title.

If you would like to know more about becoming a **Reader Ambassador** for *Love & Justice,* please email us at blackbird.digibooks@gmail.com and we'll let you know how you can become a valuable, visible, part of this book's journey to a wider audience

http://blackbird-books.com
@blackbirdebooks
A publishing company for the digital age
We publish rights-reverted and new titles by established quality writers alongside exciting
new talent.

blackbird